A Guide to Computing Statistics with SPSS® 11 for Windows

With Supplements for Releases 8, 9 and 10

Revised Edition

DENNIS HOWITT AND DUNCAN CRAMER

Prentice
Hall

An imprint of Pearson Education

Harlow, England · London · New York · Reading, Massachusetts · San Francisco
Toronto · Don Mills, Ontario · Sydney · Tokyo · Singapore · Hong Kong · Seoul
Taipei · Cape Town · Madrid · Mexico City · Amsterdam · Munich · Paris · Milan

Pearson Education Limited
Edinburgh Gate
Harlow
Essex CM20 2JE
England

and Associated Companies throughout the world

Visit us on the World Wide Web at:
www.pearsoneduc.com

First published 2001
Revised edition 2003

ISBN 0 131 39983 7

British Library Cataloguing-in-Publication Data
A catalogue record for this book can be obtained from the British Library

Library of Congress Cataloging-in-Publication Data
A catalog record for this book can be obtained from the Library of Congress

10 9 8 7 6 5 4 3 2
06 05 04 03 02

Typeset by 65
Printed in Great Britain by Henry Ling Limited, at the Dorset Press,
Dorchester, DT1 1HD

Contents

Preface

■ This Guide is a stand-alone practical approach to statistical analysis using *SPSS 11 for Windows* (and Releases 8, 9 and 10). It is suitable for students and researchers wishing to analyse psychological, sociological, criminological, health and similar data.

■ It gives the fastest possible access to computerised data analysis using SPSS. Users with little or no previous computer skills will quickly be able to analyse quite complex data and understand the results of the computer analysis. To this end the text describes the procedures in a step-by-step fashion which leave no doubt as to what to do next.

■ Most chapters have a common pattern which lists the order of key pressing necessary to obtain the statistical analysis but also explains how to interpret and report the SPSS output. The common structure is:

- A short introduction to the statistical techniques covered in the chapter. This includes an explanation of what the analysis does as well as suggestions about when each technique is used. For many users, especially those with a smattering of statistical knowledge, this will be sufficient background for them to get started.

- Simple examples are given of the appropriate sorts of data for each statistical technique. These examples allow users to work through our computations before moving on to their own data with confidence.

- A quick summary of the major steps in the computer analysis is given for each statistical technique. These *Quick Summaries* are intended as memory aids for those who have used the procedures before. In other words, they save time when users are already familiar with the material.

- The way in which data for a particular statistical analysis are entered into the data spreadsheet is presented visually and explained in the text.

- A step-by-step description of how a particular statistical analysis is done using SPSS for Windows is given in detail.

- The chapters include numerous examples of SPSS screens at different stages of the analysis. These screen shots are not simply informative but offer reassurance to users that they are following the steps properly.
- The SPSS statistical output is included exactly as it appears on the monitor screen and printout of the analysis. This is crucial – SPSS output can be confusing and unclear at first.
- The key features of the statistical output are listed together with simple explanations of what the important parts of the output mean.
- Recommendations are made about reporting the statistical findings in reports, theses and publications. These includes hints about how to describe research findings and how to present clear tables.

■ *Statistical Package for the Social Sciences* (SPSS) was initially developed in 1965 at Stanford University in California. It is the leading data analysis package in the field and available all over the world in universities and elsewhere. Modern computing developments have enabled its use on home computers. Because of its popularity and universality, using SPSS is one of the most readily transferable of all research skills. Once SPSS has been learnt it can be used practically anywhere. Furthermore, SPSS is constantly being updated so that up-to-date statistics will be included in each new version.

■ SPSS now uses the *Windows* operating system for personal computers. *Windows* employs a system of *menus* and *dialog boxes*. In the interest of simplicity, and because they are sufficient for the vast majority of users, we have confined our coverage to menus and dialog boxes alone. The big advantage of menus is that the options can be seen on the screen and do not need to be remembered or a manual constantly referred to. The alternative is to enter typed commands or instructions. The problem with these is that SPSS syntax can be a little difficult to master. However, readers who have used the pre-Windows versions of SPSS may already be familiar with the syntax and so will find its use easy. Most users of SPSS for Windows will find in the windows and dialog boxes all the facilities that they require.

■ This Guide is based on the latest versions of *SPSS for Windows* (i.e. Releases 10 and 11); but remains suitable for Releases 8 and 9 because of their similarity. Supplements are provided which describe the main differences in Releases 8, 9 and 10. Although SPSS is updated every few years, usually there is little difficulty in adapting knowledge gained on the older versions to the new version.

■ Finally, a few things should be mentioned about this guide as a resource for learning, teaching, and research:

- The Guide is not a complete statistics textbook. Some readers will benefit from studying any of the many statistics textbooks alongside this Guide. Such textbooks provide detailed conceptual and theoretical background to the statistical techniques. The Guide is intended as a practical resource dealing with the business of getting data analysed and understood quickly. As such, readers at all levels should find it useful no matter their level of statistical sophistication.

- This Guide can be used alongside virtually any statistics textbook to support a wide variety of statistics and practical courses. The range of statistical techniques covered is large and includes the simplest as well as the most important of the advanced statistical techniques. The variety of techniques described and the relative ease of using SPSS for Windows ensure that the Guide can be used at introductory, intermediate and advanced levels of statistics teaching.

- The structure of the Guide is such that statistical procedures are described more-or-less in order of conceptual difficulty. Generally speaking, computing with SPSS is equally easy for advanced statistical techniques as it is for simple ones.

- Chapter 1 is essential reading, as it explains data entry and basic computer operations. However, the remaining chapters can be used on a stand-alone basis if necessary. Users with insufficient time to work chapter-by-chapter through the Guide should find enough detail in the relevant chapters to complete an SPSS analysis successfully. At the end of Chapter 1 Table 1.3 states which chapter is most appropriate for which purpose, thereby enabling the reader to move directly to that part of the book.

- Those wishing to work steadily through the book will profit by doing so. They will have a much better overview of SPSS computing procedures. For most readers, this is possible in a matter of hours especially when they have prior knowledge of statistics.

- SPSS has an extensive catalogue of statistical procedures – far more than can be included in a short Guide like this. We have provided sound choices suitable for most purposes when the range of possibilities is likely to confuse the average reader. The quickness and ease of SPSS mean that more advanced users can explore the alternatives with the use of menus and dialog boxes without wasting too much time. Most users should find our coverage more than sufficient.

- The data and statistical analyses carried out in this book correspond almost always to those in the authors' own accompanying statistics text, *An Introduction to Statistics for Psychology* (2002) published by Prentice Hall. This book is referred to as *ISP*, followed by the corresponding table number.

Chapter 1

How to access SPSS Releases 10 and 11 for Windows and enter data

■ *This chapter gives an overview of the basic operation of SPSS for Windows. It includes data entry as well as saving data as files. It is essential preparation for the later chapters for readers with no previous experience of earlier versions of SPSS for Windows.*

1.1   Introduction

SPSS Releases 10 and 11 for Windows are accessed on a personal computer (or PC for short). A PC consists of five major components (Figure 1.1):

1.   a television-like *screen* (also called a *monitor* or *visual display unit*) to display information;

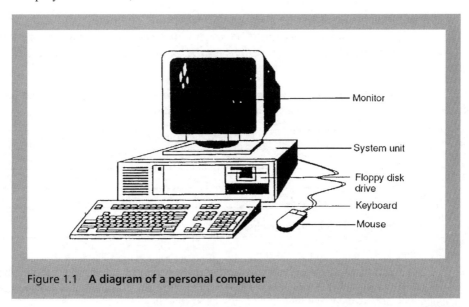

Figure 1.1   **A diagram of a personal computer**

2.   a *keyboard* to type in information;

3.   a *system unit* which houses the computer itself and usually a *drive* for inserting a *floppy disk*;

4.   a *printer* to print information that you have produced;

5.   usually a small hand-held 'switch' called a *mouse*.

Moving the mouse on a hard surface causes the *pointer* to move on the screen. This pointer is sometimes called a *cursor*. Selecting your chosen option involves moving the pointer to cover that option on the screen. You then press or *click on* the *left* button of the mouse.

At a university, college or school, you will normally need:

1.   a personal code (or *ID*) and

2.   a *password*.

Obtain these from the appropriate individual or department (e.g. the computer centre) at your institution; the ID and password have to be typed in before you can access SPSS.

1.2   To access SPSS

■ Before switching on the computer, make sure that you remove floppy disks left in any of the disk drives. If you forget, you may have to switch off and start again.

■ Make sure that both the screen *and* the system unit are switched on. This may involve one switch or two.

■ What to do next depends on the way your computer has been set up; so precise instructions cannot be given here. They may involve more than one step; usually you have to enter your *ID* and *password*. See Table 1.1.

Table 1.1   **To remind yourself, write here the additional steps you need to take to access SPSS at your particular location**

■ _____

■ _____

■ _____

■ _____

Remember to keep your password secret!

A window of more-or-less the kind shown in Figure 1.2 should appear once you have completed the necessary steps. [The window will probably not be identical

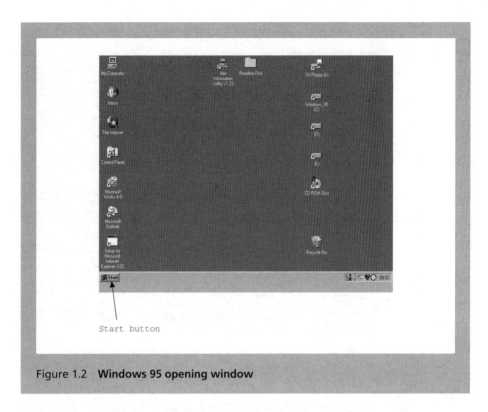

Start button

Figure 1.2   **Windows 95 opening window**

to the one in Figure 1.2. It depends on local circumstances. The rest of the screen may vary somewhat from our example, depending on how it has been set up or *configured*.]

■ Move the cursor to the ▆▆ **Start** button or *icon* at the bottom of the screen and press or click on the left button of the mouse.

■ Move the cursor to the 'Programs' option on the first menu which opens the second menu shown in Figure 1.3.

■ Move the cursor to the 'SPSS for Windows' option and then to the 'SPSS 10.0 for Windows' option (Figure 1.3). Click on this last option.

Selecting the SPSS option produces, after some seconds' delay, the Data Editor window depicted in Figure 1.4.

When SPSS is first installed, a small dialog box entitled 'SPSS for Windows' will be superimposed on the Data Window. Subsequent users, however, may have prevented this box from appearing by moving the cursor to the box beside 'Don't show this dialog in the future', clicking the left button of the mouse, moving the cursor to 'Cancel' and clicking the left button of the mouse. Because this dialog box only appears when opening SPSS and because previous users may have deleted this option, we have ignored this facility.

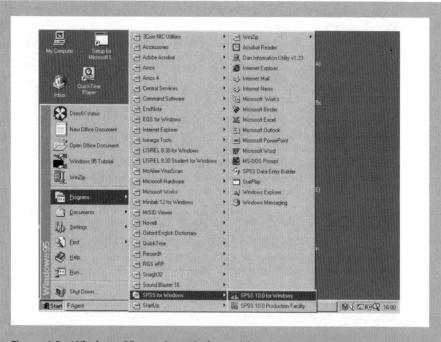

Figure 1.3   **Windows 95 opening window with Program Manager menus**

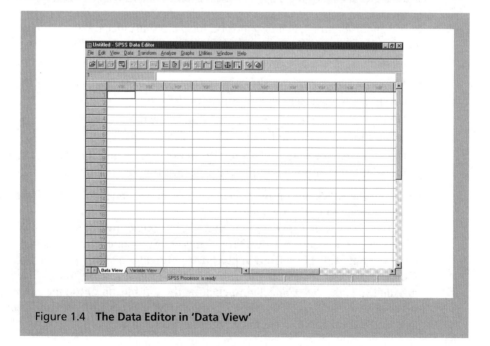

Figure 1.4   **The Data Editor in 'Data View'**

It is generally easier to work with windows opened to their maximum. If the Data Editor does not occupy most of the screen, move the cursor to the icon in the extreme top left corner of the Data Editor beside 'Untitled – SPSS Data Editor' and click on the left button of the mouse, which will produce a drop-down menu. Move the cursor to 'Maximise' and click the left button of the mouse. This procedure can be used for other windows as well.

The Data Editor consists of two windows. Which window is displayed depends on which window was showing when SPSS was previously closed down and is indicated at the bottom left hand corner. Data needs to be entered in the Data View window shown in Figure 1.4, so click on the Data View tab at the bottom left of the screen if necessary. The Variable View window is displayed in Figure 2.4 and is initially described in Chapter 2.

1.3   To enter data

Data are put in the Data Editor window. We will enter the ages of fifteen university students as given in Table 1.2.

Table 1.2   **Fifteen numerical scores**

18	21	23	18	19	19	19	33	18	19	19	20	18	19	18

Quantitative data are normally organised in terms of the columns and rows of a table:

1. Different columns represent different variables such as age and sex in SPSS.
2. Different rows represent the data for different cases. In psychology a case is usually a person.

Because age is our only variable, only one column is needed for the fifteen values. We will use the first column to contain the age scores but any column could be used.

The *cell* in the first row of the first column is *framed in bold* (Figure 1.4). The bold frame denotes where the datum will go once it has been typed in on the keyboard and the *Return* or *Enter* key pressed.

■ Type in the first number, 18, on the keyboard.

■ Press Return or Enter. 18 will be placed in the first cell after a short delay. Wait until the number appears in the cell before typing in the next number.

■ The name of the column will change from 'var' to 'var00001' and the bold frame of the cell will move to the next cell below (i.e. the cell in the second row of the first column).

■ If the bold frame does not move to the next cell, use either the mouse (see section 1.4) or the cursor key with the downward-pointing arrow on it ↓ (see section 1.5) to move it.

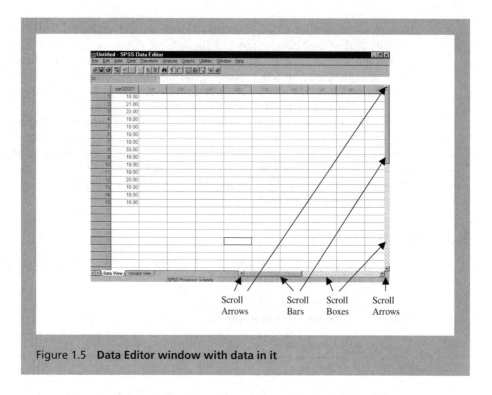

Figure 1.5   **Data Editor window with data in it**

■ This new cell is now active. Type in all 15 values (Figure 1.5).

Note that the values are to two decimal places. SPSS does this automatically or by *default* unless you instruct it otherwise. In this case, age is a whole number, so the two decimal places will remain as zeros and have no effect.

Mistakes in the Data Editor

If you type in the wrong numbers then a) move the cursor to that cell and b) type in the right values.

If you forget to put in a row, such as missing out the value of 21 in the second row of the Data Editor, then a) move the cursor to that cell and press the left button; b) move the cursor to the 'Data' option on the *menu bar* towards the top of the screen and press the left button, which produces a *drop-down* menu (Figure 2.2); c) move the cursor to the 'Insert Case' option on this drop-down menu and press the left button; d) type in the correct value (e.g. 21); and press the 'Return' key.

1.4   Moving within a window with the mouse

Note also that (on a 14 inch screen) there is more information in the Data Editor window than is visible at any one time:

■ To move or to *scroll* vertically use the *vertical scroll bar* (Figure 1.5).

■ To scroll horizontally use the *horizontal scroll bar* (Figure 1.5).

The position of the scroll bar or box (Figure 1.5) indicates your relative position in the window. For example, if the scroll box is at the top of the scroll bar (as it is in Figure 1.4), you are at the top of the window. If the scroll box is lower down the scroll bar (as it is in Figure 1.5), you will be lower down the window.

■ To scroll one row at a time, place the cursor on the *scroll arrow* pointing in the direction you want to go and press the left mouse button once.

For example, to move down a row at a time, place the cursor on the downward-pointing arrow (or below the scroll box) and press the left mouse button.

■ You can also *drag* the scroll box to the position in the window you want by placing the cursor on it, pressing the left mouse button without releasing it, moving the cursor to the desired position, and then releasing the button.

1.5   Moving within a window by using keyboard keys

You can scroll within a window by using the *cursor keys* (on the keyboard) which, as their name implies, affect the cursor. Although you can manage without most of them, check the following keyboard keys to see their functions:

■ The left-facing arrow ← moves the cursor one space or character to the left whereas the right-facing arrow → moves the cursor one space or character to the right.

■ The upward-facing arrow ↑ moves the cursor one line up and the downward-facing arrow ↓ one line down.

■ Press the 'Home' key to move the cursor to the beginning of the line it is on and the 'End' key to move the cursor to the end containing information on that line.

■ Press the 'PgUp' (Page Up) key to move the cursor up one screen or page at a time.

■ Press the 'PgDn' (Page Down) key to move it down one screen at a time.

■ Holding down the 'Ctrl' (Control) key *and* pressing the 'Home' key moves the cursor to the top left of the window.

■ Holding down the 'Ctrl' key *and* pressing the 'End' key moves the cursor to the bottom left of the window.

1.6   To save data

Data are stored in *files*. Saving your data in files ensures that you do not waste time retyping them. Files can be stored:

1.   on the *hard disk* of the system unit and/or

2.   on a *floppy disk* placed in the disk drive.

Saving at least one copy of your file onto a floppy disk in case the file in your PC is deleted is a smart move.

You must use a floppy disk *formatted* for your computer. If the floppy disk is new, first format it for your PC. If the floppy disk has already been formatted, make sure that the format is compatible with your PC. If it is not, re-format it. Many floppy disks are sold already formatted.

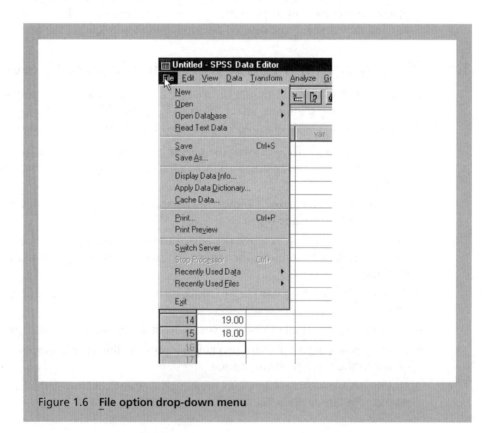

Figure 1.6   **File option drop-down menu**

Data are usually stored in a *system* file. Files are given names which consist of

1. a prefix (or *stem*) of up to eight characters followed by a full stop. The stem name usually refers to the content of the file (such as age in our example),

2. a suffix or *extension* of three characters. The extension name refers to the type of file. The extension name automatically given to system files (i.e. by *default*) is 'sav'.

Consequently we could call our file 'age.sav'. You retrieve the file for later use with its file name.

Perform the following steps to save the data as a system file on a floppy disk in disk drive 'a':

■ Move the cursor to the 'File' option on the *menu bar* near the top of the window and select it to give a *drop-down* menu (Figure 1.6).

■ Move the cursor to the 'Save As . . .' option and select it to produce the 'Save Data As' dialog box (Figure 1.7).

■ In the box beside 'File name:', type the disk drive name followed by a colon 'a:', the file stem name 'age' and the file extension name '.sav' so that the file name reads 'a:age.sav'. It is not essential to add the extension name as this is done automatically. Extension names are usually represented by icons and not words (see Figure 1.8).

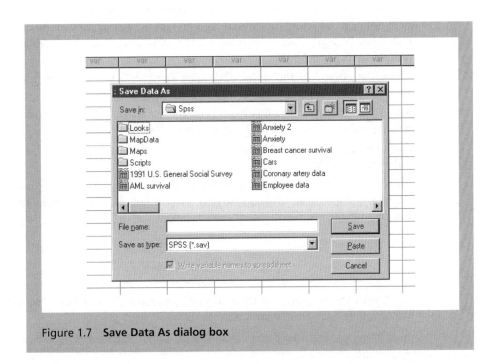

Figure 1.7   **Save Data As dialog box**

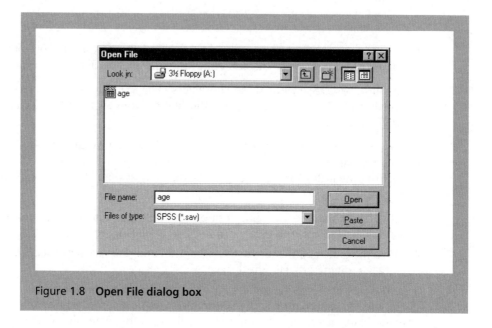

Figure 1.8   Open File dialog box

■ Move the cursor to the button labelled 'Save' and select it. The data have now been saved as a system file named 'age.sav' on the floppy disk in the disk drive called 'a'. To retrieve this file from a floppy disk in disk drive 'a', carry out the following steps.

■ Move the cursor to the 'File' option on the menu bar near the top of the window, which gives a drop-down menu (Figure 1.6).

■ Move the cursor to the 'Open . . .' option from the 'File' drop-down menu, which produces the 'Open File' dialog box (Figure 1.8).

■ Click on 'age' in the box under 'Look in:', which puts 'age' in the box beside 'File name:' as shown in Figure 1.8.

■ Move the cursor to the button labelled 'Open' and select it. This operation closes the 'Open File' dialog box and, after a few moments, opens the Data Editor with the data in it.

If you wish to use another drive such as 'c', just type 'c' instead of 'a' so that the complete file name reads 'c:age.sav'.

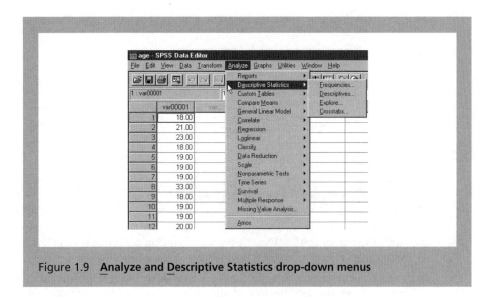

Figure 1.9   **Analyze and Descriptive Statistics drop-down menus**

1.7   Running a simple statistical procedure

■ To carry out a statistical procedure, move the cursor to the 'Analyze' option on the menu bar near the top of the screen, which gives a drop-down menu listing the various statistics options (left menu in Figure 1.9).

■ To conduct a simple procedure such as finding the mean of a set of scores, move the cursor to the 'Descriptive Statistics' option, which gives a drop-down menu listing the options available (right menu in Figure 1.9).

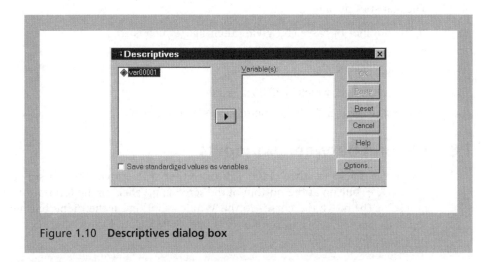

Figure 1.10   **Descriptives dialog box**

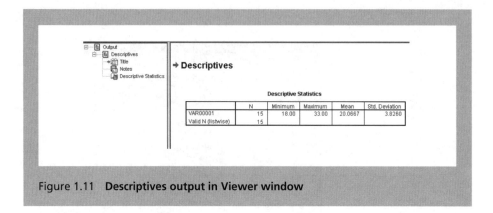

Figure 1.11   **Descriptives output in Viewer window**

■ Move the cursor to the 'Descriptives . . .' option and click on the left button of the mouse. This opens the 'Descriptives' dialog box (Figure 1.10).

■ Move the cursor to the right-facing arrow ▶ in the 'Descriptives' dialog box and click on the left button of the mouse. This puts 'var00001' in the box under 'Variable(s):' (Figure 1.10).

■ Move the cursor to 'OK' in the dialog box and click the left button on the mouse. This produces the default descriptives statistics shown in Figure 1.11 in the Viewer window.

Note that if the window is divided as shown in Figure 1.11, the left section (called the *outline pane*) is generally not needed. It can be hidden by clicking on the window divider and moving the divider to the left margin of the window by 'pulling' it to the left with the mouse button still clicked on. The outline pane lists the SPSS operations carried out in a session. Note also that the vertical scroll bar only appears when there is more than a screen's worth.
The statistics displayed are:

■ the number of cases (N) giving their age, which is 15;

■ the minimum age, which is 18.00 years;

■ the maximum age, which is 33.00;

■ the mean age, which is 20.0667; and

■ the standard (Std) deviation of age, which is 3.8260.

1.8   Moving between windows

To move back to the Data Editor either (a) move the cursor to the age - S... button at the bottom of the screen and click on the left button of the mouse or (b) move the cursor to the Window option on the menu bar near the top of the screen, move the cursor to '1 age – SPSS Data Editor' and click the left button of the mouse.

1.9   Clearing the Data Editor

■ If you want to put a new set of data in the Data Editor (such as the data described in the next chapter), clear the data already entered by moving the cursor on to the 'File' option on the menu bar near the top of the screen and select it, which produces a drop-down menu (Figure 1.6).

■ Move the cursor onto the 'New' option on this drop-down menu and select it, which produces a second drop-down menu.

■ Move the cursor on to the 'Data' option on this second drop-down menu, which will clear the data in the Data Editor. You can now type in a new set of data.

1.10 Printing output

■ One way of printing the information when it is displayed in the Viewer window is to select the material you want printed. Obviously a printer has to be properly installed already.

■ Select 'Edit', which produces a drop-down menu (Figure 1.12).

■ Select 'Select', which displays a second drop-down menu (Figure 1.12).

■ Select 'Last Output' (Figure 1.12), which puts a box around the title of the table and the table (Figure 1.13).

■ Select 'File', which produces a drop-down menu (Figure 1.6).

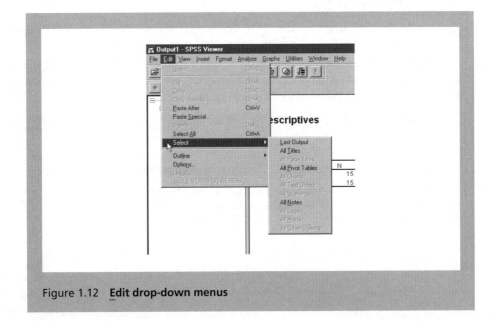

Figure 1.12   **Edit drop-down menus**

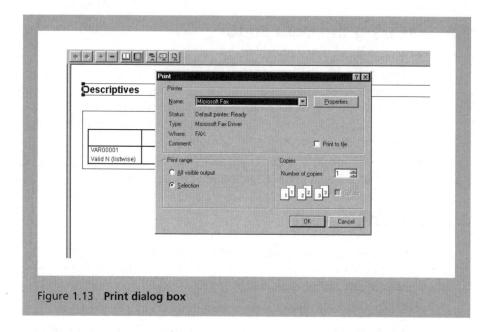

Figure 1.13 **Print dialog box**

- Select 'Print . . .', which produces the 'Print' dialog box (Figure 1.13).
- Select 'OK' to print out the selected section.

1.11 To leave SPSS

- Move the cursor to the 'File' option on the menu bar near the top of the screen and select it to display the drop-down menu (Figure 1.6).
- Move the cursor to the 'Exit' option (Figure 1.6) when a small dialog box (Figure 1.14) will be shown. Alternatively, move the cursor to the eXit button in the top right corner of the screen and click.

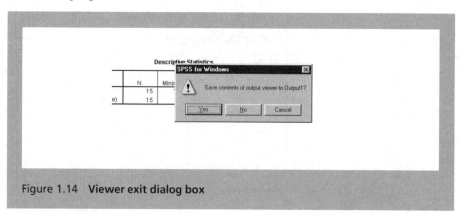

Figure 1.14 **Viewer exit dialog box**

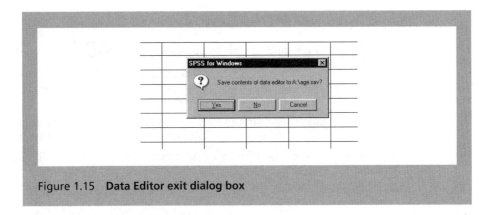

Figure 1.15   Data Editor exit dialog box

- As we do not want to save the contents of the Viewer we select 'No'. This produces another small dialog box (Figure 1.15).

- As we have already saved the contents of the Data Editor we select 'No' and we exit from SPSS.

> You cannot break a computer by experimenting with the mouse and key-board. So newcomers to computers might care to play for a minute or two to develop their skills. If by any chance things 'lock up' – that is pressing the keys or mouse has no effect – simply switch off. You will have to start again from scratch, however, if this happens. Wait 15 seconds before doing this.

1.12 Using this book

Generally speaking, once you have worked through the material in the present chapter, you should be able to follow the computations in the remaining chapters. Since descriptive statistics on each of your variables are required in any statistical analysis, we would recommend that you familiarise yourself with the procedures in Chapters 2, 3, 4 and 5. These chapters also explain how to label variables and values of variables.

Remember that most statistical analyses use numerical measurements or scores which indicate the quantity of a characteristic (variable) for each of your cases. Far fewer statistical analyses use variables which involve merely allocating individuals to named categories and summing the frequencies of cases in each category. The main statistical techniques which use data in the form of frequencies are pie-diagrams and bar charts (Chapter 2); the mode (Chapter 3); cross-tabulation tables and compound/ stacked bar charts (Chapter 6); Chi-square, the Fisher test and the McNemar test (Chapter 14), Coefficient Kappa (Chapter 30) and Log-linear (Chapter 31).

Table 1.3 **Major types of analysis and suggested SPSS procedures**

Type/purpose of analysis	Suggested procedures	Location
All types of study	Descriptive statistics Tables Diagrams	Chapters 2, 3, 4 and 5
Assessing the relationship between two variables	Correlation coefficient Regression	Chapter 6 Chapter 7
Comparing two sets of scores for differences	Unrelated *t*-test *F*-ratio test Related *t*-test Unrelated ANOVA Related ANOVA Mann–Whitney Wilcoxon Matched Pairs	Chapter 13 Chapter 19 Chapter 12 Chapter 20 Chapter 21 Chapter 18 Chapter 18
Comparing the means of two or more sets of scores	Unrelated ANOVA Related ANOVA Multiple-comparisons	Chapter 20 Chapter 21 Chapter 23
Complex experiments etc. with TWO or more independent variables and ONE dependent variable	2 (or more)-way ANOVA	Chapter 22
– if you have related AND unrelated measures	Mixed-design ANOVA	Chapter 24
– if other variables may be affecting scores on dependent variable	Analysis of covariance	Chapter 24
Eliminating third variables which may be affecting a correlation coefficient	Partial correlation	Chapter 26
Finding predictors for a variable	Simple regression Stepwise multiple regression Hierarchical multiple regression Log-linear analysis	Chapter 7 Chapter 28 Chapter 29 Chapter 31
Analysing a questionnaire	Factor analysis Alpha reliability Split-half reliability Recoding Computing new variables	Chapter 27 Chapter 30 Chapter 30 Chapter 16 Chapter 17
Comparing frequency data	Chi-square Fisher test McNemar test	Chapter 14 Chapter 14 Chapter 14
Coding open-ended data using raters	Kappa coefficient	Chapter 30

All other techniques require all variables to be measured as numerical scores. The exception to this is experimental designs such as those requiring the Analysis of Variance. These require the dependent variable to be measured as a numerical score whereas the independent variable consists of a small number of categories which may sometimes imply numerical order or size. When numerical scores can be placed into a small number of categories, some researchers use techniques such as Chi-square and cross-tabulation tables for their analysis.

Finally, it is important to note that any variable which has only two measured categories (dichotomous variables) may be treated as a numerical score. Thus a variable such as sex which is measured as either male or female may use the numeric codes 1 and 2. These numeric codes can then be used as numeric scores. These dichotomously coded variables can then be used in the Pearson correlation coefficient, factor analysis and virtually any other statistical analysis. Table 1.3 gives some hints as to the appropriate SPSS analyses for different types of data analysis.

Chapter 2

Describing variables: tables and diagrams

■ *Clear and meaningful tables and diagrams are crucial in statistical analysis and report writing. Virtually every analysis of data uses them in order to allow the distributions of variables to be examined. In this chapter we provide the basic computer techniques to allow the construction of tables and diagrams to describe the distributions of individual variables presented one at a time.*

■ *Frequency tables merely count the number of times different values of the variable appear in the data. This may be as simple as a count of the number of males and the number of females in the research. Tables need to be relatively simple and this usually requires a small number of different values of the variable or a number of different values grouped together.*

■ *Pie-diagrams are effective and simple ways of presenting frequency counts of this sort. However, they are only useful when the variable in question has a small number of different values. Because they consume space they are not very common in books and journals although they are good for conference presentations and lectures.*

■ *A bar chart can be used in similar circumstances to the pie chart and can cope with a larger number of values of variables. Frequencies in categories are presented as physically separated bars of varying height.*

■ *A histogram is similar to a bar chart except it is used when the variable consists of numerical scores. Thus the bars in a histogram are presented in size order of the scores that they represent. The bars in histograms are NOT separated by spaces. Often a histogram will need the ranges of scores covered by each bar to be changed in order to achieve a sensible and useful diagram. This could be done by recoding variables (Chapter 16) but SPSS also allows this to be done in the Chart Editor.*

SPSS is generally used to summarise raw data but it can use data which have already been summarised such as those shown in Table 2.1 (*ISP* Table 2.1).

Table 2.1   **Occupational status of participants in the research expressed as frequencies and percentage frequencies**

Occupation	Frequency	Percentage frequency
Nuns	17	21.3
Nursery teachers	3	3.8
Television presenters	23	28.8
Students	20	25.0
Other	17	21.3

In other words, since the data in Table 2.1 are based on 80 people, the data would occupy 80 cells of one column in the Data Editor window and each occupation would be coded with a separate number so that Nuns might be coded 1, Nursery teachers 2, and so on. Thus, one would need 17 rows containing 1 to represent Nuns, 3 rows containing 2 to represent Nursery teachers, and so on. However, it is possible to carry out certain analyses on summarised data provided that we appropriately weight the categories by the number or frequency of cases in them.

2.1   Weighting categories

(Skip this section if you are using raw data)

Quick summary

Enter a code for each category in the first column of Data Editor

Enter frequency of cases in second column

Data

Weight Cases . . .

Weight cases by

var00002

▶

OK

■ We need to give a different numerical code to each of the five categories or groups in Table 2.1. So we will call Nuns 1, Nursery teachers 2, and so on. Each of the first five cells in the first column of the Data Editor will contain one of these codes as shown in Figure 2.1.

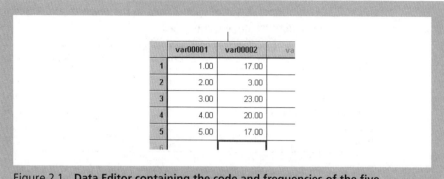

Figure 2.1   **Data Editor containing the code and frequencies of the five occupational categories**

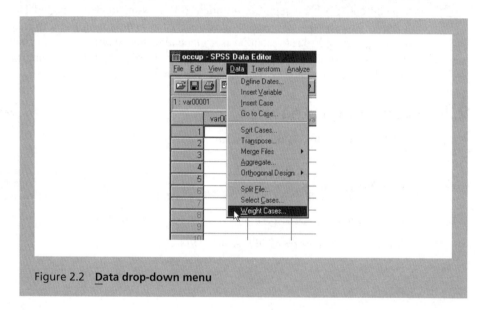

Figure 2.2   **Data drop-down menu**

- The second column will contain the frequency of the five occupational groups.
- Select 'Data' from the menu bar near the top of the screen, which produces a drop-down menu (Figure 2.2). (Moving the cursor to a particular option and clicking on that option is referred to as 'Select', i.e. in this case 'select the Data option' or more simply as 'select Data'.)
- Select 'Weight Cases . . .' from this drop-down menu, which opens the Weight Cases dialog box (Figure 2.3).
- Select 'Weight cases by'.
- Select 'var00002' and then the ▶ button, which puts 'var00002' in the 'Frequency Variable:' text box.

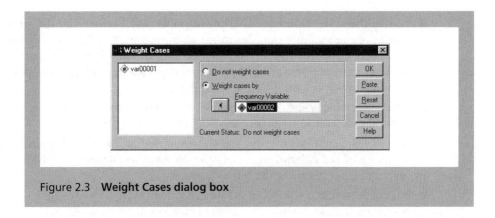

Figure 2.3   **Weight Cases dialog box**

■ Select 'OK', which closes the Weight Cases dialog box. The five cells are now weighted by the numbers in the second column. 'Weight on' appears at the bottom right of the Data Editor window

2.2   Labelling variables and their values

Quick summary

Variable View in Data Editor

Row to be labelled (e.g. first row)

Brief name under Name (e.g. occupat)

Longer name under Label (e.g. Occupation)

Cell under Values

. . .

Value: box

Numerical code (e.g. 1)

Value Label: box

Label (e.g. Nuns)

Add

Repeat as necessary

OK

■ You will find it helpful to label the variable and each of the different categories of the variable in order to avoid confusion. The following procedure does this for the five codes in the first column of Data Editor. We will generally label variables and sometimes their categories throughout the book. This is good practice if a little time-consuming.

■ Select 'Variable View' which displays the window shown in Figure 2.4. This shows the default settings for the variables.

■ To make the columns narrower as shown in Figure 2.4, select the line next to the name of the column whose width you want to change (e.g. 'Name') and move the column line to the left as desired.

■ Select the variable you want to label (e.g. 'var00001') by moving to it in the 'Name' column and typing in a label of no more than eight characters. We will call 'var00001' 'occupat' by typing in 'occupat' which will delete the default name 'var00001' in the 'Name' column (Figure 2.6). This name will appear at the top of the first column in 'Data View'.

■ SPSS names must begin with an alphabetic character (A–Z). The remaining characters can be any letter, number, period, @ (at), $ (dollar) or _ (underscore). Blank spaces are not allowed and they cannot end with a period and preferably not with an underscore. In addition certain words, known as *keywords*, cannot be used because they can only be interpreted as commands by SPSS. They include words such as **add**, **and**, **any**, **or**, and **to**, to give but a few examples. No keyword contains numbers so you can be certain that names which include numbers will always be recognized as such. You cannot use the same name twice. SPSS will tell you if you break any of these rules and will not allow you to proceed.

■ We can provide a longer version of this name by moving to the first row under 'Label' and typing 'Occupation' (Figure 2.6). This name will appear first when listed in dialog boxes (Figure 2.7) followed by the shorter name in brackets. It will be the only name appearing in the output (Table 2.2) and reminds us what an abbreviated name is.

Figure 2.4   **Data Editor in 'Variable View' (with columns narrowed and default settings for variables)**

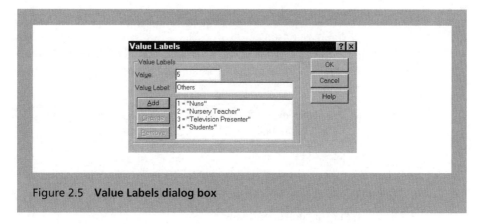

Figure 2.5   **Value Labels dialog box**

■ To label the values of a variable, select the appropriate cell in the 'Values' column. This displays three dots known as an ellipse (Figure 2.6).

■ Select this ellipse which opens a dialog box called 'Value Labels' (Figure 2.5).

■ Select box beside 'Value:' and type 1 in it.

■ Select box beside 'Value Label:' and type Nuns in it.

■ Select 'Add', which puts 1.00 = "Nuns" in the bottom box.

■ Repeat this procedure for the remaining four values and labels as shown in Figure 2.5.

■ Select 'OK', which closes the Value Labels dialog box.

■ Label the second column 'Freq' for the short label and 'Frequencies' for the longer label (Figure 2.6).

2.3   Omitting decimal places in whole numbers

Quick summary

Variable View in Data Editor

Row/variable under Decimals (e.g. first row)

Downward arrow twice

■ The data you will be entering for the exercises in this book consist of whole numbers. Consequently, having two zero decimal places is unnecessary and may be visually distracting. The number of decimal places shown in the Data Editor may be changed with the following procedure which we shall use throughout the book.

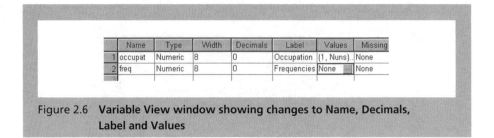

Figure 2.6   **Variable View window showing changes to Name, Decimals, Label and Values**

■ Select the first row under 'Decimals' in the 'Variable View' window.
■ Click twice on the downward arrow which decreases 2 to 0 (Figure 2.6).
■ Do the same for the second row.

2.4   Percentage frequencies

Quick summary

A̲nalyze

D̲escriptive Statistics

F̲requencies . . .

Column variable (e.g. Occupation)

OK

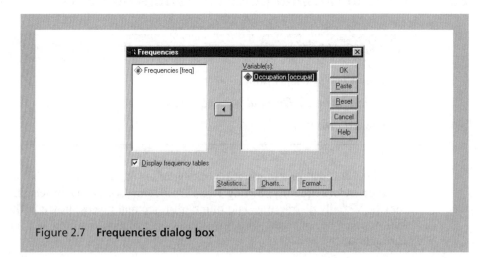

Figure 2.7   **Frequencies dialog box**

■ Select 'Analyze' on the menu bar near the top of the window, which produces a drop-down menu (Figure 1.9).

■ Select 'Descriptive Statistics', which displays a second drop-down menu which is positioned to the right of the first drop-down menu in Figure 1.9.

■ Select 'Frequencies . . .' which opens the Frequencies dialog box (Figure 2.7).

■ Select 'Occupation(occupat)' and the ▶ button, which puts 'Occupation (occupat)' in the 'Variable[s]:' text box.

■ Select 'OK', which closes the Frequencies dialog box and the Data Editor window and which displays the output shown in Table 2.2 in the Viewer window.

Table 2.2   **Frequency table produced by the Frequency procedure**

Statistics

Occupation

N	Valid	80
	Missing	0

Occupation

		Frequency	Percent	Valid Percent	Cumulative Percent
Valid	Nuns	17	21.3	21.3	21.3
	Nursery Teachers	3	3.8	3.8	25.0
	Television Presenters	23	28.8	28.8	53.8
	Students	20	25.0	25.0	78.8
	Other	17	21.3	21.3	100.0
	Total	80	100.0	100.0	

2.5   Interpreting the output in Table 2.2

■ The first table presents the number of valid cases, which is 80.

■ The second table presents frequency statistics for the five categories of Occupation.

■ Column 1: The value labels are listed, Nuns, Nursery Teachers, etc.

■ Column 2: The frequency of each of the categories is presented. Thus there are 17 cases which have the value label 'Nuns'.

■ **Column 3: The percentage of cases in each category for the sample as a whole is displayed**. This includes any values that you may have defined as missing values of which there are none in this example. Thus 21.3% of the cases in the sample are coded as 'Nuns'.

■ Column 4: The percentage of cases in each category for the sample excluding any missing values is presented. Since there were no values defined as missing in our example, columns 3 and 4 are identical. (See Chapter 15.)

■ Column 5: The cumulative percentage excluding any missing values is found in the final column of numbers. Thus 78.8% of the cases were students, television presenters, nursery teachers or nuns.

2.6   Reporting the results in Table 2.2

■ Table 2.1 presents most of the main features of these data. It can be used as a model. Extend it if necessary to include more information.

■ Be wary of reporting all of the SPSS output since there is a certain amount of 'overkill'. It may be sufficient to report the data shown in Table 2.1.

■ Avoid SPSS specific terms especially 'valid percent'.

2.7   Pie-diagram of category data

Quick summary

Graphs

Pie . . .

Define

Slice variable (e.g. Occupation)

% of cases

OK

■ If using the Weight Cases procedure, make sure that the procedure is still in operation by checking for 'Weight on' in the bottom right of the Data Editor window.

■ Select 'Graphs' on the menu bar near the top of the window, which displays a drop-down menu (Figure 2.8). Note that it is not necessary to return to the Data Editor to carry out further statistical procedures.

■ Select the 'Pie . . .' option, which opens the Pie Charts dialog box (Figure 2.9).

■ Select 'Define', which opens the 'Define Pie: Summaries for Groups of Cases' sub-dialog box (Figure 2.10).

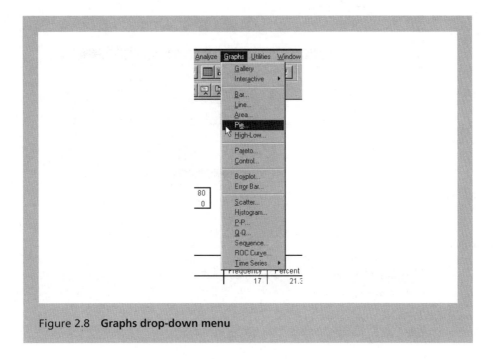

Figure 2.8   **Graphs drop-down menu**

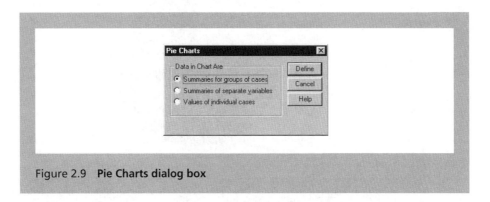

Figure 2.9   **Pie Charts dialog box**

■ Select 'Occupation(occupat)' and then the ▶ button, which puts 'Occupation(occupat)' in 'Define Slices by:' text box as shown in Figure 2.10.

■ Select '% of cases'.

■ Select 'OK', which closes the 'Define Pie: Summaries for Groups of Cases' sub-dialog box and the Data Editor window and which displays the pie-diagram shown in Figure 2.11 in the Viewer window.

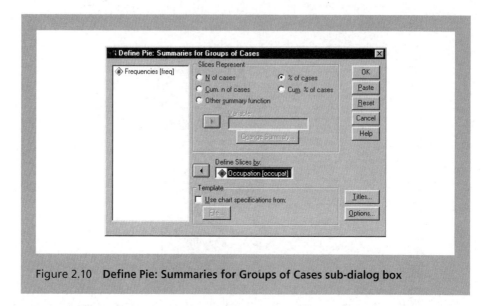

Figure 2.10   **Define Pie: Summaries for Groups of Cases sub-dialog box**

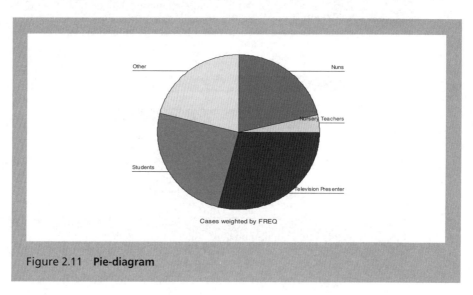

Figure 2.11   **Pie-diagram**

2.8   Editing the pie chart

It is possible to edit the pie-diagram. Its initial appearance depends partially on what options have been selected by the previous user of the SPSS program. Because of space limitations, we will illustrate the way in which just two specific aspects of the pie-diagram can be changed: moving the labels to the outside of the pie-diagram and changing the colour of a slice to a black and white pattern.

There are others aspects you may wish to modify which you should be able to discover by trying out other options.

2.9   Moving labels to the outside of the pie-diagram

Quick summary

Double click on figure

Chart

Options . . .

Percents

Format

Box beside Position

Outside

Continue

Change first slice position if necessary

OK

Chart Window icon

Close

■ In Figure 2.11, part of the labels 'Nursery Teachers' (i.e. 'Nursery') and 'Television Presenters' (i.e. 'T') are inside the pie-diagram, making these labels slightly more difficult to read. To ensure that the labels are outside the pie-diagram, carry out the following procedure.

■ Note also that the maximum length of the name displayed in figures and diagrams is 20 characters so that the 's' of 'Television Presenters' is omitted. In this case the name could be shortened to 'TV Presenters'.

■ Move the cursor anywhere inside the square containing the pie-diagram in the Viewer window and double click on the left button of the mouse. This opens up the Chart Editor window as shown in Figure 2.12.

■ Select 'Chart' on the menu bar in the Chart Editor window, which produces a drop-down menu (Figure 2.13).

■ Select 'Options . . .' on this drop-down menu, which opens the Pie Options dialog box (Figure 2.14).

■ Select 'Percents' (Figure 2.14).

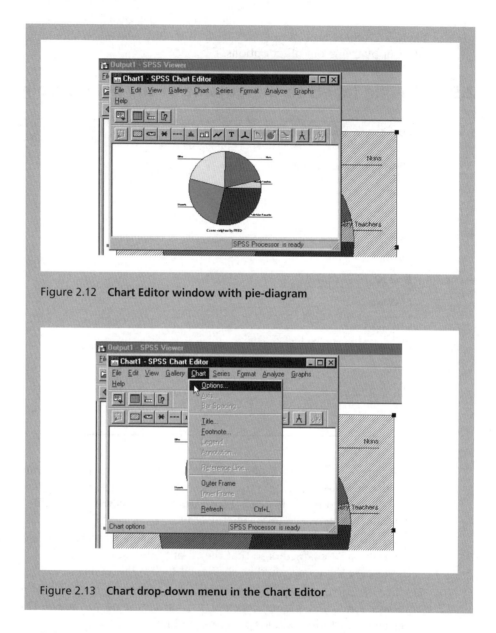

Figure 2.12   **Chart Editor window with pie-diagram**

Figure 2.13   **Chart drop-down menu in the Chart Editor**

■ Select 'Format . . .' which opens the 'Pie Options: Label Format' sub-dialog box (Figure 2.15).

■ Select the box beside 'Position', which produces a drop-down menu and select 'Outside' (Figure 2.15).

■ Select 'Continue', which closes the 'Pie Options: Label Format' sub-dialog box.

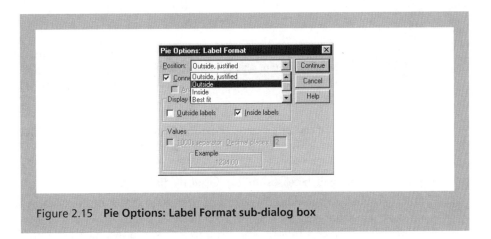

Figure 2.14   **Pie Options dialog box**

Figure 2.15   **Pie Options: Label Format sub-dialog box**

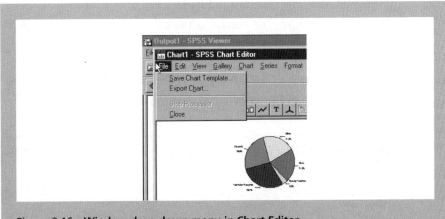

Figure 2.16   **Window drop-down menu in Chart Editor**

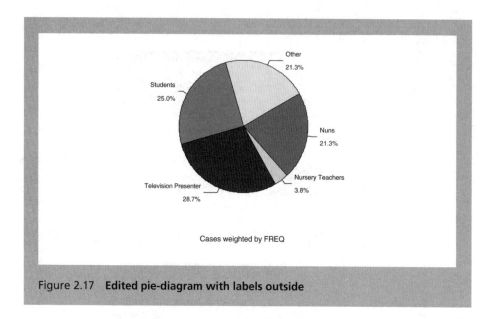

Figure 2.17   **Edited pie-diagram with labels outside**

■ Highlight '12' in the box beside 'Position First Slice at:' and type 2 to turn the pie-diagram to ensure that there is sufficient space to display 'Nursery Teachers'.

■ Select 'OK', which closes the Pie Options dialog box.

■ To go back to the edited version of the pie-diagram in the Viewer window, select the Chart Editor window icon in the top left corner of the menu bar of the Chart Editor window. This produces a drop-down menu (Figure 2.16).

■ Select 'Close' from this menu to close the Chart Editor (Figure 2.16). The edited pie-diagram is shown in Figure 2.17.

■ Alternatively, move the cursor to the eXit button in the top right corner of this window and click.

2.10 Changing the colour of a pie-diagram slice to a black and white pattern

Quick summary

Figure in Chart Editor

Slice

Format

Fill Pattern . . .

Pattern

Apply

Repeat as necessary

Close

Format

Color . . .

Slice

New colour (e.g. white)

Apply

Repeat as necessary

Close

■ With the pie-diagram in the Chart Editor as shown in Figure 2.18, click the left button of the mouse once to select the slice to be changed (e.g. 'Students').

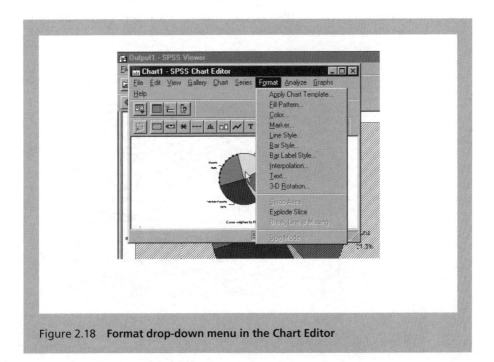

Figure 2.18   **Format drop-down menu in the Chart Editor**

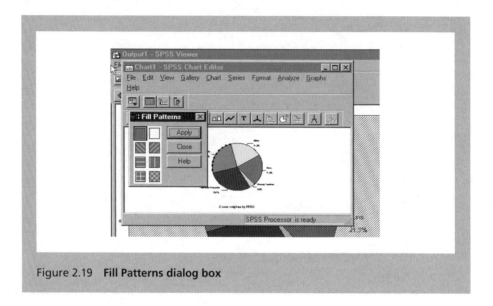

Figure 2.19 **Fill Patterns dialog box**

■ Select 'Format' on the menu bar of the Chart Editor window which produces a drop-down menu (Figure 2.18).

■ Select 'Fill Pattern . . .', which opens the Fill Patterns dialog box (Figure 2.19).

■ Select a pattern and then select 'Apply', which applies the chosen pattern to the slice.

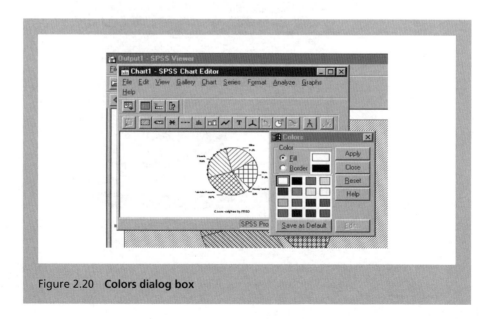

Figure 2.20 **Colors dialog box**

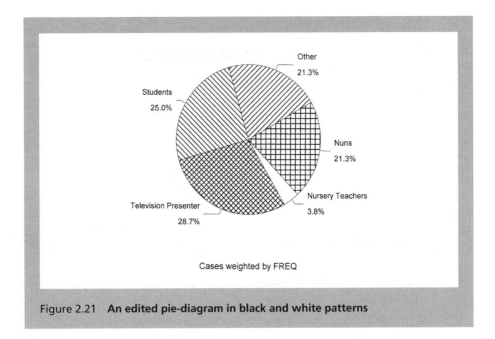

Figure 2.21   **An edited pie-diagram in black and white patterns**

■ Move the cursor onto another slice, select it and apply another pattern. Do this for all five slices. Select 'Close' to close the Fill Patterns dialog box.

■ Select 'Format' on the menu bar of the Chart Editor window, which produces a drop-down menu (Figure 2.18).

■ Select 'Color . . .' which opens the Colors dialog box (Figure 2.20).

■ Select each slice in turn and apply the colour white. Close the Colors dialog box and the Chart Editor. An example of a pie-diagram in black and white patterns is shown in Figure 2.21.

2.11 Bar chart of category data

Quick summary

Graphs
Bar . . .
Define
Variable (e.g. Occupation)
% of cases
OK

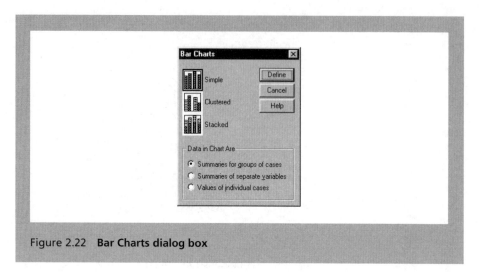

Figure 2.22   **Bar Charts dialog box**

■ If using the Weight Cases procedure, make sure that the procedure is still in operation.

■ Select 'Graphs', which produces a drop-down menu (Figure 2.8).

■ Select 'Bar . . .' which opens the Bar Charts dialog box (Figure 2.22).

■ Select 'Define', which produces the 'Define Simple Bar: Summaries for Groups of Cases' sub-dialog box (Figure 2.23).

■ Select 'Occupation(occupat)' and then the ▶ button beside the 'Category Axis:' text box, which puts 'Occupation(occupat)' in this box as shown in Figure 2.23.

■ Select '% of cases'.

■ Select 'OK', which closes the 'Define Simple Bar: Summaries for Groups of Cases' sub-dialog box and the Data Editor window and which displays the bar chart (Figure 2.24) in the Viewer window.

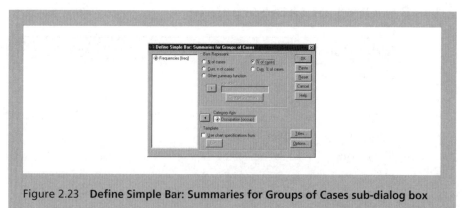

Figure 2.23   **Define Simple Bar: Summaries for Groups of Cases sub-dialog box**

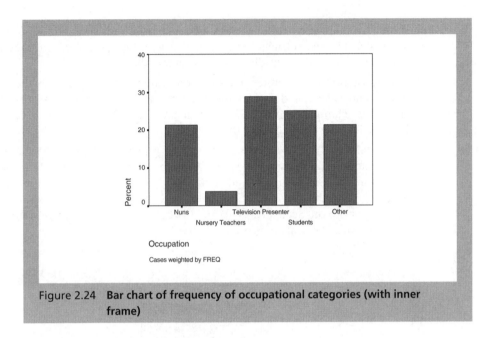

Figure 2.24   **Bar chart of frequency of occupational categories (with inner frame)**

2.12 Adding/removing grid lines and frames

Quick summary

Chart Editor
Chart
Inner Frame
Chart
Axis
Scale
OK
Grid
OK
Chart
Axis
Category
OK
Grid lines
OK

■ If the bar chart you produce looks different from that shown in Figure 2.24, this is because the settings have been changed. For example, you may have horizontal and vertical gridlines and no inner frame.

■ To add or remove an inner and/or outer frame, select 'Chart' in the Chart Editor and select or de-select the appropriate option from the drop-down menu. For example, Figure 2.13 shows that an Outer Frame has been selected. To de-select this, just click on this option.

■ It may take a little practice to change other aspects in the bar chart. We will show you how to add grid lines as these are absent from Figure 2.24. Select 'Chart' in the Chart Editor and then 'Axis . . .' from the drop-down menu which displays the Axis Selection dialog box shown in Figure 2.25. You need to change both the Scale (vertical) and Category (horizontal) axes in turn. We will start with the Scale axis first.

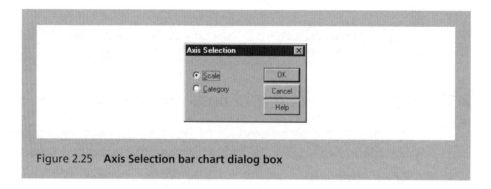

Figure 2.25   **Axis Selection bar chart dialog box**

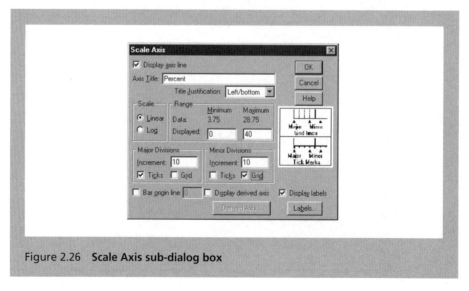

Figure 2.26   **Scale Axis sub-dialog box**

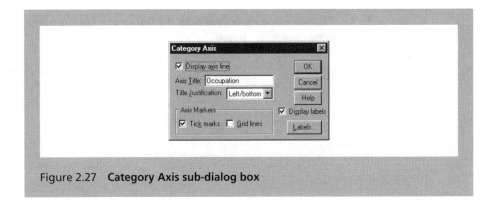

Figure 2.27   **Category Axis sub-dialog box**

■ Select 'OK' which produces the 'Scale Axis' sub-dialog box shown in Figure 2.26.

■ Select 'Grid and then 'OK'. Horizontal grid lines should appear across the bar chart in the Chart Editor.

■ Do the same for the Category axis. Select 'Chart' in the Chart Editor and then 'Axis . . .'. Select Category in the Axis Selection dialog box (Figure 2.25). Select 'OK' which produces the Category Axis sub-dialog box shown in Figure 2.27. Select 'Grid lines' and then 'OK'. Vertical gridlines now also appear across the bar chart.

2.13 Histograms

Quick summary

Graphs

Histogram . . .

Column variable (e.g. response)

OK

We will illustrate the making of a histogram with the data in Table 2.3 which shows the distribution of students' attitudes towards statistics. Enter the data in the Data Editor and weight and label them as described at the beginning of this chapter (we have labelled this variable 'response').

■ Select 'Graphs', which produces a drop-down menu (Figure 2.8).

■ Select 'Histogram . . .' which opens the Histogram dialog box (Figure 2.28).

Table 2.3   **Distribution of students' replies to the statement 'Statistics is my favourite university subject'**

Response category	Value	Frequency
Strongly agree	1	17
Agree	2	14
Neither agree nor disagree	3	6
Disagree	4	2
Strongly disagree	5	1

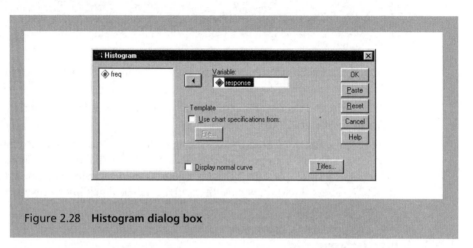

Figure 2.28   **Histogram dialog box**

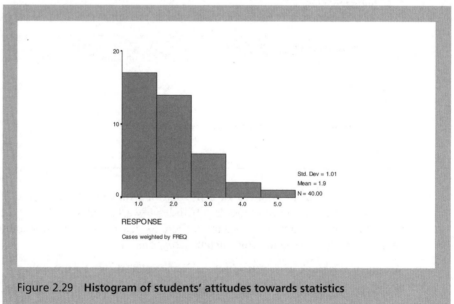

Figure 2.29   **Histogram of students' attitudes towards statistics**

■ Select 'response' and then the ▶ button, which puts 'response' in the 'Variable:' text box as shown in Figure 2.28.

■ Select 'OK', which closes the Histogram dialog box and the Data Editor window and which displays the histogram presented in Figure 2.29 in the Viewer window.

■ Use 'Format' in the Chart Editor to change the colour and fill pattern as was shown for the pie chart (see section 2.10).

2.14 Editing histograms

■ Although this works fine with our example, sometimes your histogram will not be ideal. You can change the number and size of the intervals along the base of the histogram as follows.

■ With the histogram in the Chart Editor, select 'Chart' which produces a drop-down menu (Figure 2.13).

■ Select 'Axis' which opens the Axis Selection dialog box as shown in Figure 2.30.

■ Select 'Interval' (Figure 2.30).

■ Select 'OK', which opens the 'Interval Axis' sub-dialog box as shown in Figure 2.31.

■ Select 'Custom' (Figure 2.31).

■ Select 'Define . . .', which opens the 'Interval Axis: Define Custom Interval' sub-dialog box as shown in Figure 2.32.

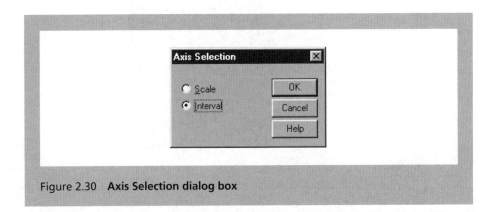

Figure 2.30   **Axis Selection dialog box**

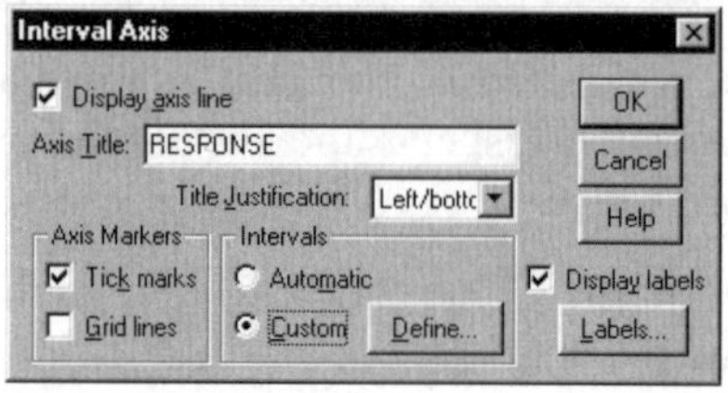

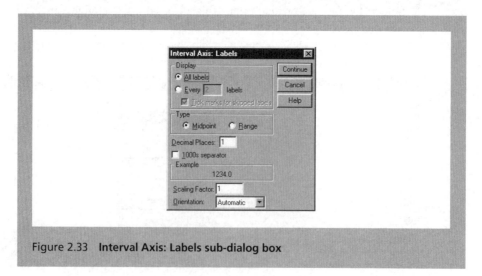

Figure 2.31   Interval Axis sub-dialog box

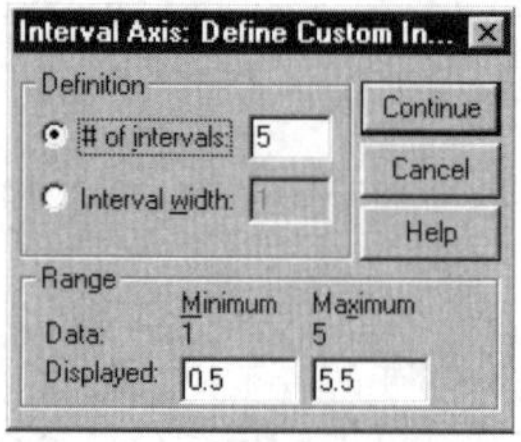

Figure 2.32   Interval Axis: Define Custom Interval sub-dialog box

Figure 2.33   Interval Axis: Labels sub-dialog box

■ In the Definition section you can alter the number of intervals required ('# of intervals:') and the width of the intervals ('Interval width'), while in the Range section you can alter the 'Minimum' and 'Maximum' values.

■ In the 'Interval Axis' sub-dialog box, you can select 'Labels . . .', which opens the 'Intervals Axis: Labels' sub-dialog box as shown in Figure 2.33.

■ These procedures need a trial-and-error approach, as they are very flexible.

■ The best choices for editing your charts are contained in the 'Chart' and 'Format' options of the menu bar of the Chart Editor.

■ Usually if you double click on a part of the diagram in the Chart Editor the most useful menu for altering that part of the diagram will appear.

Chapter 3

Describing variables numerically: averages, variation and spread

- In this chapter we describe the computation of a number of statistics which summarise and describe the essential characteristics of data. The techniques presented in this chapter involve individual variables taken one at a time. In other words they are single variable or univariate statistical techniques.

- With the exception of the mode, they are only appropriate if you have data in the form of scores. The mean is simply the everyday or numerical average of a set of scores. It is obtained by summing the scores and dividing by the number of scores.

- The mode is simply the most frequently occurring score. A set of scores can have more than one mode if two or more scores occur equally frequently. The mode is the value of the score occurring most frequently – it is NOT the frequency with which the most frequent score occurs.

- The median is the score in the middle of the distribution if the scores are ordered in size from the smallest to the largest. For various reasons, sometimes the median is an estimate of the score in the middle – for example, where the number of scores is equal so that there is no exact middle.

We will illustrate the computation of the mean, median and mode on the ages of twelve university students (this guide Table 3.1; *ISP* Table 3.7):

Table 3.1 **Ages of 12 students**

18	21	23	18	19	19	19	33	18	19	19	20

Type the ages in the first column of the Data Editor. Remember to label the variable and to delete the two zero decimal places.

3.1   Descriptive Statistics

Quick summary

Analyze

Descriptive Statistics

Frequencies

Variable (e.g. age) ▶ *button*

Statistics

Mean, Median and Mode

Continue

OK

- Select 'Analyze' on the menu bar towards the top of the window, which produces a drop-down menu (Figure 1.9).
- Select 'Descriptive Statistics', which displays a second drop-down menu (Figure 1.9).
- Select 'Frequencies . . .', which opens the Frequencies dialog box (Figure 2.7).

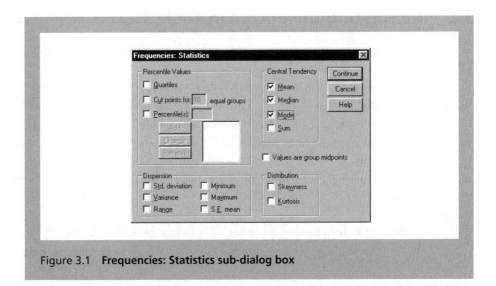

Figure 3.1   **Frequencies: Statistics sub-dialog box**

■ De-select 'Display frequencies tables', which are otherwise automatically produced and which we do not require. There is a query from the computer at
this point. Select the 'OK' button.

■ Select 'age' and the ▶ button, which puts 'age' in the 'Variable[s]:' text box.

■ Select 'Statistics', which opens a second or sub-dialog box called Frequencies:
Statistics (Figure 3.1).

■ Select 'Mean', 'Median' and 'Mode' in the section entitled Central Tendency
as shown in Figure 3.1. A tick ☑ should appear to indicate the choices you
make.

■ Select 'Continue', which closes the 'Frequencies: Statistics' sub-dialog box.

■ Select 'OK', which closes the Frequencies dialog box and the Data Editor
window and which displays the output shown in Table 3.2 in the Viewer
window.

Table 3.2   **Mean, median and mode produced by the Frequencies procedure**

Statistics

AGE

N	Valid	12
	Missing	0
Mean		20.50
Median		19.00
Mode		19

3.2   Interpreting the output in Table 3.2

■ The output gives us the following information about the age of this group of
university students:

(a)   The mean age in the group is 20.50 years (i.e. the average age).

(b)   The median age in the group is 19.00 years (i.e. the age of the person in
the middle of the distribution ordered from youngest to oldest).

(c)   The modal age in the group is 19 years (the most frequently occurring
age).

■ By comparing these three measures of central tendency, it looks like the
distribution is not symmetrical as they all differ. This can be confirmed by
looking at Table 3.1.

■ The output tells us that there are 12 Valid cases and 0 Missing cases:

(a)   The Valid cases is the number of ages which have been included in the
analysis. In this case it equals the number of scores in Table 3.1.

(b) The Missing cases is the number of scores which have been disregarded for the purposes of the analysis. Do not let this worry you; as long as the Missing cases = 0 then there is no problem. (SPSS allows you to identify particular values of a variable as 'missing'. If the computer comes across these for a particular variable, they will be disregarded for analysis purposes. The only circumstances in which this will happen is if you have specifically identified certain values that you want ignoring (see Chapter 15) or if any cells in the Data Editor contain a dot (.).

3.3 Reporting the output in Table 3.2

■ The mean, median and mode can be presented as a table such as Table 3.3.

■ Two decimal places are more than enough for most data. Most measurement is approximate, and the use of several decimal places tends to imply an unwarranted degree of precision.

■ For the median, it is probably less confusing if you do not report values as 19.00 but as 19. However, if the decimal places were anything other than .00 then this should be reported since it indicates that the median is estimated and does not correspond to any actual scores.

Table 3.3 **Mean, median and mode of age**

Ages of students (N = 12)	
Mean	20.50 years
Median	19 years
Mode	19 years

3.4 Other features

You will see from Figure 3.1 that in the sub-dialog box there are many additional statistical values which may be calculated. You should have little difficulty obtaining these by adapting the steps already described.

Percentiles – indicate the cutoff points for percentages of scores. Thus the ninetieth percentile is the score which cuts off the bottom 90% of scores in terms of size.

Quartiles – values of a distribution which indicate the cutoff points for the lowest 25%, lowest 50%, and lowest 75% of scores.

Sum – the total of the scores on a variable.

Skewness – frequency distributions are not always symmetrical about the mean. Skewness is an index of the asymmetry or lop-sidedness of the distribution of scores on a variable. It takes a positive value if the values are skewed to the left and a negative value if they are skewed to the right.

Kurtosis – an index of how much steeper or flatter the distribution of scores on the variable is compared to the normal distribution. It takes a '+' sign for steep frequency curves and a '−' sign for flat curves.

Standard deviation (estimate) – this is a measure of the amount by which scores differ on average from the mean of the scores on a particular variable. Its method of calculation involves unusual ways of calculating the mean. In SPSS the standard deviation is calculated as an estimate of the population standard deviation. It is an index of the variability of scores around the mean of a variable. Some authors call this the sample standard deviation.

Variance (estimate) – this is a measure of the amount by which scores on average vary around the mean of the scores on that variable. It is the square of the standard deviation and is obviously therefore closely related to it. It is also always an estimate of the population variance in SPSS. Some authors call this the sample variance. Like standard deviation, it is an index of the variability of scores around the mean of a variable but also has other uses in statistics. In particular, it is the standard unit of measurement in statistics.

Range – the numerical difference between the largest and the smallest scores obtained on a variable. It is a single number.

Minimum (score) – the value of the lowest score in the data for a particular variable.

Maximum (score) – the value of the highest score in the data for a particular variable.

Standard error (SE mean) – the average amount by which the means of samples drawn from a population differ from the population mean. It is calculated in an unusual way. Standard error can be used much like standard deviation and variance as an index of how much variability there is in the scores on a variable.

Chapter 4

Shapes of distributions of scores

- ■ *It is important to study the shape of the distribution of scores on a variable. Ideally for most statistical techniques, a distribution should be symmetrical and normally distributed (bell-shaped).*
- ■ *Researchers should be wary of very asymmetrical (skewed) distributions and distributions which contain a few unusually high or low scores (outliers). Histograms, for example, can be used to detect asymmetry and outliers.*

We will compute a frequency table and histogram of the extraversion scores of the 50 airline pilots shown in Table 4.1 (*ISP* Table 4.1).

Table 4.1   **Extraversion scores of 50 airline pilots**

3	5	5	4	4	5	5	3	5	2
1	2	5	3	2	1	2	3	3	3
4	2	5	5	4	2	4	5	1	5
5	3	3	4	1	4	2	5	1	2
3	2	5	4	2	1	2	3	4	1

4.1   Frequency tables

Quick summary

Enter the data

Analyze

Descriptive Statistics

Frequencies

Select variable ▶ *button*

OK

- As described in Chapter 1, enter the extraversion scores in the first column of the Data Editor window. Label the variable (e.g. 'extrav') and remove the two zero decimal places.
- Save the data, as described in Chapter 1, in a system file called 'ext.sav'.
- Select 'Analyze', which produces a drop-down menu (Figure 1.9).
- Select 'Descriptive Statistics', which displays a second drop-down menu (Figure 1.9).
- Select 'Frequencies . . .', which opens the Frequencies dialog box (Figure 2.7).
- Select 'extrav' (if you have only one variable this will already be highlighted for you) and then the ▶ button, which puts 'extrav' in the 'Variable[s]:' text box.
- Select 'OK', which closes the Frequencies dialog box and the Data Editor window and which displays the output shown in Table 4.2 in the Viewer window.

Table 4.2   **Frequency table of extraversion scores of 50 airplane pilots as produced by Frequencies**

Statistics

EXTRAV

N	Valid	50
	Missing	0

EXTRAV

		Frequency	Percent	Valid Percent	Cumulative Percent
Valid	1	7	14.0	14.0	14.0
	2	11	22.0	22.0	36.0
	3	10	20.0	20.0	56.0
	4	9	18.0	18.0	74.0
	5	13	26.0	26.0	100.0
	Total	50	100.0	100.0	

4.2   Interpreting the output in Table 4.2

■ Column 1: The five categories of extraversion scores are listed in the left-most column of numbers. They are 1, 2, 3, 4 and 5.

■ Column 2: The frequency of each of these categories is to be found here. Thus there are 10 cases with an extraversion value of 3.

■ Column 3: The percentage of cases in each category for the sample as a whole. This includes any values that you may have defined as missing values. Thus 20% of the cases in the sample are in the 3 category.

■ Column 4: The percentage of cases in each category for the sample excluding any missing values. Since there were no values defined as missing in our example, columns 3 and 4 are identical.

■ Column 5: The cumulative percentage excluding any missing values is found in the final column of numbers. Thus 74% of the cases had a value of 4 or less.

4.3   Reporting the output of Table 4.2

Table 4.3   One style of reporting output in Table 4.2

Extraversion score	Frequency	Percentage frequency	Cumulative percentage frequency
1	7	14.0	14.0
2	11	22.0	36.0
3	10	20.0	56.0
4	9	18.0	74.0
5	13	26.0	100.0

Notice that we omitted some of the confusion of detail in Table 4.2. Tables and diagrams need to clarify the results.

4.4   Histograms

Quick summary

Enter the data or retrieve file

Graphs

Histogram

Select variable (e.g. 'extrav') ▶ *button*

OK

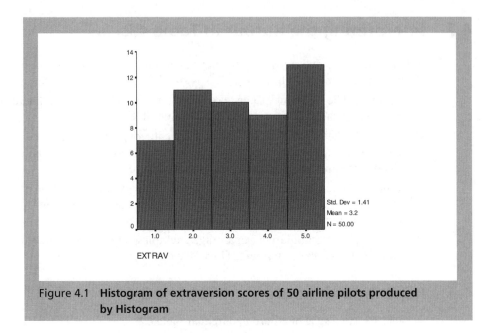

Figure 4.1 **Histogram of extraversion scores of 50 airline pilots produced by Histogram**

■ Select 'Graphs', which produces a drop-down menu (Figure 2.8).

■ Select 'Histogram . . .', which displays the Histogram dialog box (Figure 2.15).

■ Select 'extrav' (which will already be highlighted for you if you only have one variable) and then the ▶ button which puts 'extrav' in the 'Variable:' text box.

■ Select 'OK', which closes the Histogram dialog box and the Data Editor window and which displays the output shown in Figure 4.1 in the Viewer window.

■ This histogram can be edited by putting it in the Chart Editor (see section 2.14). Examples of the results of such editing can be seen in Figure 4.2.

4.5 Interpreting the output in Figure 4.1

■ The horizontal axis of this histogram gives the values 1.0, 2.0, 3.0, 4.0 and 5.0. These are the five different values of extraversion scores in Table 4.1.

■ The vertical axis gives frequencies of individuals or cases from 0 to 14 in steps of two.

■ The heights of the bars tell you how frequent each extraversion score is in the data.

■ Std.Dev = 1.41 is the value of the standard deviation. This is discussed again in Chapter 5 of this book.

■ The average of the fifty extraversion scores is given by Mean = 3.2.

■ N = 50.00 means that the number of scores = 50.

4.6   Reporting the output in Figure 4.1

- Although Figure 4.1 may be easily interpreted by you, it is not suitable for inclusion unmodified in your reports.
- The vertical axis needs to be labelled 'f' or 'frequencies'.
- The horizontal axis needs to be labelled 'extraversion scores'.
- Figure 4.2 contains the additional information needed.

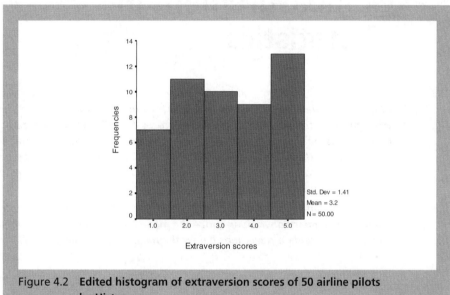

Figure 4.2   **Edited histogram of extraversion scores of 50 airline pilots by Histogram**

Chapter 5

Standard deviation: the standard unit of measurement in statistics

■ Basically, standard deviation is an index of how much scores deviate (differ) 'on average' from the average of the set of scores of which they are members. In other words, standard deviation is an index of the amount of variability of scores around the mean of the scores. Standard deviation can also be used in order to turn scores on very different variables into z- or 'standard scores' which are easily compared and summed.

■ Standard deviation always takes a positive value BUT researchers write of a number of standard deviations above the mean (i.e. '+' relative to the mean) or a number of standard deviations below the mean (i.e. '−' relative to the mean).

We shall illustrate the computation of the standard deviation and z-scores with the nine age scores shown in Table 5.1 (based on *ISP* Table 5.1).

Table 5.1 **Data for the calculation of standard deviation**

Age	20	25	19	35	19	17	15	30	27

5.1 Standard deviation

Quick summary

Analyze

Descriptive Statistics

Descriptives

Select variables ▶

Options

Std deviations

Continue

OK

■ Enter the data into the Data Editor, label the variable (e.g. 'age') and remove the two zero decimal places.

■ Select 'Analyze', which produces a drop-down menu (Figure 1.9).

■ Select 'Descriptive Statistics', which displays a second drop-down menu (also Figure 1.9).

either

■ Select 'Frequencies . . .' and follow the procedure described in Chapter 3, selecting 'Std deviation' in the 'Frequencies: Statistics' sub-dialog box (Figure 3.1).

or

■ Select 'Descriptives . . .', which opens the Descriptives dialog box (Figure 1.10).

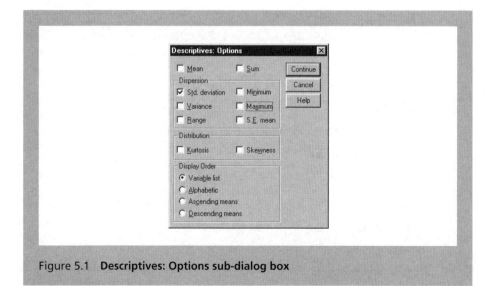

Figure 5.1   **Descriptives: Options sub-dialog box**

■ Select 'age' and then the ▶ button, which puts 'age' in the 'Variable[s]:' text box.

■ Select 'Options . . .', which opens the 'Descriptives: Options' sub-dialog box (Figure 5.1).

■ Select 'Std deviations' and de-select 'Mean', 'Minimum' and 'Maximum' by clicking off these options (if you only want standard deviations). Normally you will find the mean and minimum plus maximum useful.

■ Select 'Continue', which closes the 'Descriptives: Define' sub-dialog box.

■ Select 'OK', which closes the Descriptives dialog box and Data Editor window and which displays the output shown in Table 5.2 in the Viewer window.

Table 5.2   **Standard deviation of nine ages as produced by Descriptives**

Descriptive Statistics

	N	Std. Deviation
AGE	9	6.65
Valid N (listwise)	9	

5.2   Z-scores

Quick summary

Analyze

Descriptive Statistics

Descriptives

Select 'Save standardized values as variables'

Select variables ▶

Options

Std deviations

Continue

OK

Figure 5.2 **z-scores produced by Descriptives and displayed in the Data Editor**

This involves just one extra step:

■ To obtain z-scores we simply select 'Save standardized values as variables' in the Descriptives dialog box (Figure 1.10), which will put the z-scores in the next column in the Data Editor entitled 'zage' as shown in Figure 5.2.

In other words, for each of your scores the z-score has been calculated and placed in a separate column in your data window. This new 'variable' will be lost unless you save your data before ending the session.

5.3   Interpreting the output in Table 5.2

■ The standard deviation of the nine ages is 6.65. This is the 'average' amount by which each score deviates from the mean score in the set. Standard deviation is quite a complex concept so refer to ISP Chapter 5 if you have any difficulties or another textbook.

■ The standard deviation is based on nine valid cases. In other words, the computer has not found any values of age which you previously have defined as 'missing' or to be ignored (Chapter 15).

5.4   Reporting the output in Table 5.2

■ The standard deviation of just one variable can easily be mentioned in the text of your report: "It was found that the standard deviation of age was 6.65 years (N = 9)."

■ However, it is more likely that you would wish to record the standard deviation alongside other statistics such as the mean and range, as illustrated in Table 5.3. You probably wish to include these statistics for other numerical score variables that you have data on.

Table 5.3 **The sample size, mean, range and standard deviations of age, IQ and verbal fluency**

	N	Mean	Range	Standard deviation
Age	9	23.00	20.00	6.65
IQ	9	122.17	17.42	14.38
Verbal fluency	9	18.23	4.91	2.36

5.5 Other features

'Descriptives' contains a number of statistical calculations which are easily selected. These different statistical concepts are briefly explained at the end of Chapter 3.

Mean
Sum
Standard deviation (estimate)
Range
Minimum (score)
Maximum (score)
Standard error (S.E. mean)
Kurtosis
Skewness

Chapter 6

Relationships between two or more variables: diagrams and tables

■ *A great deal of research explores the relationship between two or more variables. While the univariate (single-variable) statistical procedures described so far have their place in the analysis of practically any data, many research questions require methods which help assess the interrelationships or correlations between different variables in addition.*

■ *As with univariate statistics, a thorough statistical analysis of data requires an exploration of the basic trends in the data by the use of tables and diagrams. These methods include cross-tabulation tables, compound histograms (clustered bar charts) and scattergrams. Most of these are familiar to many of us.*

■ *Care has to be taken to make sure that the tables and diagrams you obtain are useful and communicate well. In particular, ensure that your data for cross-tabulation tables and compound histograms (clustered bar charts) only contain a small number of different data values. If they do not, SPSS will produce massive tables and dense unreadable graphs and diagrams.*

■ *Scattergrams, on the other hand, also work well when you have many different values for the scores on your variables.*

■ *Remember that the effective presentation of basic descriptive statistics requires that the researcher considers their tables and diagrams carefully. Often the researcher will have to 'tweak' things to make the finished tables and graphs effective forms of communication. That this can be done quickly is one of the advantages of using SPSS.*

We will illustrate the drawing up of a cross-tabulation table and compound bar chart with the data shown in Table 6.1 (*ISP* Table 6.4). This shows the number of men and women in a study who have or have not been previously hospitalised.

Table 6.1   **Cross-tabulation table of sex against hospitalisation**

	Male	Female
Previously hospitalised	F = 20	F = 25
Not previously hospitalised	F = 30	F = 14

6.1   Weighting data, labelling variables and values, and setting decimal places to zero

Quick summary

Enter code for rows in first column

Label variable and values and remove decimal places

Enter code for columns in second column

Label variable and values and remove decimal places

Enter frequencies in third column

Label variable and remove decimal places

Data

Weight Cases . . .

Weight cases by

'freq'

OK

■ We need to identify each of the four cells in Table 6.1. The rows of the table represent whether participants have been hospitalised while the columns represent the sex of the participants. We will then weight each of the four cells of the table by the number of cases in them.

■ As shown in Figure 6.1, the first column of data in the Data Editor window contains the code for whether participants have been previously hospitalised (1) or not (2).

	hospital	gender	freq	var
1	1	1	20	
2	1	2	25	
3	2	1	30	
4	2	2	14	
5				

Figure 6.1 **Weighted data in the Data Editor**

- As described in Chapter 2 (section 2.2), label this variable as 'hospital' for the short form and 'Hospitalisation' for the long form. Label the value of 1 as 'Hospitalised' and the value of 2 as 'Not hospitalised'.
- Also as described in Chapter 2 (section 2.3), set the decimal places to zero.
- The second column contains the code for males (1) and females (2).
- Label this variable as 'Gender'. Label the value of 1 as 'Male' and the value of 2 as 'Female'.
- Set the decimal place to zero.
- The third column has the frequency of people in each of these four cells.
- Label this variable as 'Freq' and set the decimal places to zero.
- Select 'Data' from the menu bar, which produces a drop-down menu (Figure 2.2).
- Select 'Weight Cases . . .' from this drop-down menu, which opens the Weight Cases dialog box (Figure 2.3).
- Select 'Weight cases by'.
- Select 'freq' and then the ▶ button, which puts 'freq' in the 'Frequency Variable:' text box.
- Select 'OK', which closes the Weight Cases dialog box. The four cells are now weighted by the numbers in the third column.

6.2 Cross-tabulation with frequencies

Quick summary

Analyze

Custom Tables

Basic Tables . . .

Row variable (e.g. hospital)

 ▶

Column variable (e.g. gender)

▶

OK

The following three steps in bold should be followed to get to the Basic Tables dialog box for all of the analyses in this section.

■ **Select 'Statistics' on the menu bar towards the top of the window, which produces a drop-down menu (Figure 1.9).**

■ **Select 'Custom Tables' on this drop-down menu, which opens a second drop-down menu.**

■ **Select 'Basic Tables . . .' on this second drop-down menu, which opens the Basic Tables dialog box (Figure 6.2: Note this dialog box contains entries for the next two steps).**

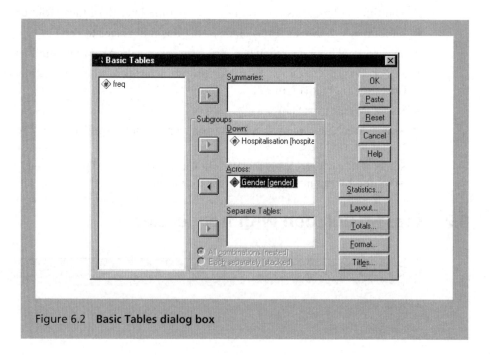

Figure 6.2   **Basic Tables dialog box**

■ If you want to put the hospitalisation variable in the rows of the table, select 'Hospitalisation(hospital)' and then the ▶ button beside the 'Down:' box, which puts 'Hospitalisation(hospital)' in this box.

■ If you want to put the gender variable in the columns of the table, select 'Gender(gender)' and then the ▶ button beside the 'Across:' box, which puts 'Gender(gender)' in this box.

■ Select 'OK', which closes the Basic Tables dialog box and the Data Editor window and which presents the output shown in Table 6.2 in the Viewer window.

Table 6.2 **Cross-tabulation table of gender against hospitalisation produced by Basic Tables**

		Gender	
		Male	Female
Hospitalisation	Hospitalised	20	25
	Not hospitalised	30	14

■ To display the frequencies in each cell as a percentage of the total, **follow the three steps in bold at the start of this section**, then select 'Statistics . . .' in the Basic Tables dialog box, which opens the 'Basic Tables: Statistics' sub-dialog box (Figure 6.3).

■ Select 'Table %' and then 'Add', which puts this term in the 'Cell Statistics' box.

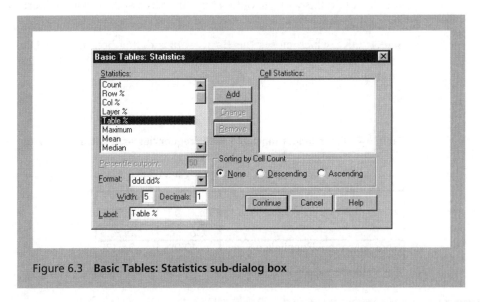

Figure 6.3 **Basic Tables: Statistics sub-dialog box**

■ Select 'Continue', which closes the 'Basic Tables: Statistics' sub-dialog box.

■ Select 'OK', which closes the Basic Tables dialog box and the Data Editor window and which presents the output shown in Table 6.3 in the Viewer window.

Table 6.3 **Cross-tabulation with frequencies as a percentage of the total**

	Gender	
	Male	Female
	Table %	Table %
Hospitalisation Hospitalised	22.5%	28.1%
Not hospitalised	33.7%	15.7%

■ To display the frequencies in each cell as a percentage of the column total, **follow the three steps in bold at the start of this section**, then select 'Statistics . . .' in the Basic Tables dialog box, which opens the 'Basic Tables: Statistics' sub-dialog box (Figure 6.3).

■ Select 'Col %' and then 'Add', which puts this term in the 'Cell Statistics' box. (If 'Table %' is still in the 'Cell Statistics' box from the previous operation, then select it and then 'Remove', which will put it back in the Statistics: box. If you do not do this you will obtain both the table and the column percentages.)

■ Select 'Continue', which closes the 'Basic Tables: Statistics' sub-dialog box.

■ Select 'OK', which closes the Basic Tables dialog box and the Data Editor window and which presents the output shown in Table 6.4 in the Viewer window.

Table 6.4 **Cross-tabulation table with frequencies as a percentage of the column total**

	Gender	
	Male	Female
	Col %	Col %
Hospitalisation Hospitalised	40.0%	64.1%
Not hospitalised	60.0%	35.9%

6.3 Compound (stacked) percentage bar chart

Quick summary

Graphs

Bar . . .

Stacked

Define

Axis variable (e.g. hospital)

Stacked variable (e.g. gender)

OK

- SPSS does not directly produce a compound (stacked) percentage bar chart in which the bars represent 100 per cent. To obtain this kind of chart indirectly you need to enter the percentage figures (called 'columper') for the two bars as shown in Figure 6.4 and weight them.
- Select 'Graphs', which produces a drop-down menu (Figure 2.8).
- Select 'Bar . . .', which opens the Bar Charts dialog box (Figure 2.12).
- Select 'Stacked'.
- Select 'Define', which produces the 'Define Stacked Bar: Summaries for Groups of Cases' sub-dialog box (Figure 6.5).

	hospital	gender	columper	var
1	1	1	40.00	
2	1	2	60.00	
3	2	1	64.10	
4	2	2	35.90	
5				

Figure 6.4 **Weighted data in the Data Editor**

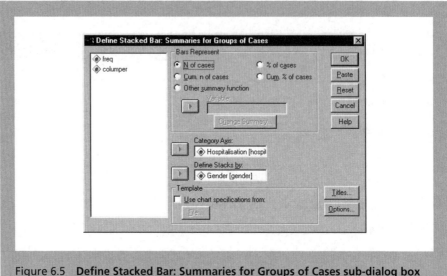

Figure 6.5   Define Stacked Bar: Summaries for Groups of Cases sub-dialog box

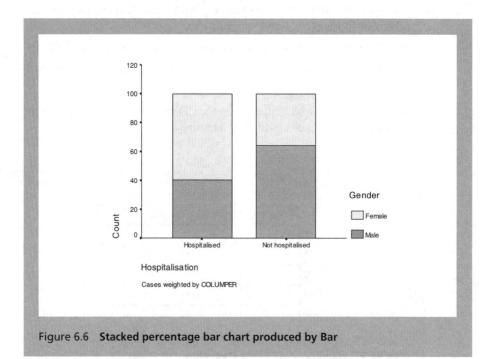

Figure 6.6   Stacked percentage bar chart produced by Bar

■ Select 'Hospitalisation(hospital)' and then the ▶ button beside the 'Category Axis:' text box, which puts 'Hospitalisation(hospital)' in this box as shown in Figure 6.5.

■ Select 'Gender(gender)' and then the ▶ button beside the 'Define Stacks by:' box, which puts 'Gender(gender)' in this box as shown in Figure 6.5.

■ Select 'OK', which closes the 'Define Stacked Bar: Summaries for Groups of Cases' sub-dialog box and the Data Editor window and which displays the stacked bar chart shown in Figure 6.6 in the Viewer window. Note that the label 'Count' on the vertical axis refers to per cent.

6.4   Changing the scale of the vertical axis to 100

Quick summary

Chart Editor

Chart

Options . . .

Change scale to 100%

OK

■ The vertical axis ranges from 0 to 120. We carry out the following procedure to change the scale to have a maximum of 100.

■ Double click on the bar to open up the Chart Editor window (e.g. Figure 2.12).

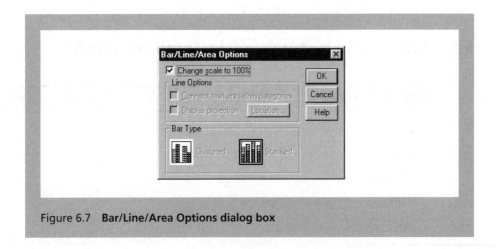

Figure 6.7   **Bar/Line/Area Options dialog box**

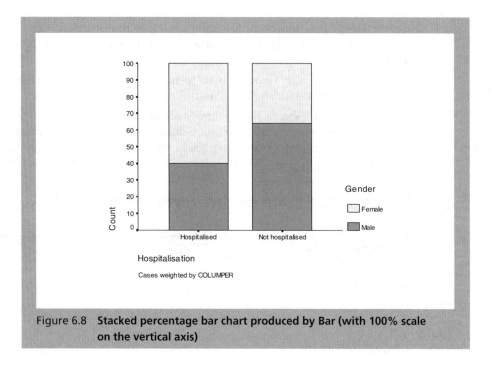

Figure 6.8   **Stacked percentage bar chart produced by Bar (with 100% scale on the vertical axis)**

■ Select 'Chart' from the menu bar of the Chart Editor window, which produces a drop-down menu (Figure 2.13).

■ Select 'Options . . .', which opens the Bar/Line/Area Options dialog box (Figure 6.7).

■ Select 'Change scale to 100%' (Figure 6.7).

■ Select 'OK' to close the Bar/Line/Area Options dialog box. Figure 6.8 shows the resulting bar chart in the Viewer window.

6.5   Compound histogram (clustered bar chart)

Quick summary

Graphs

Bar . . .

Clustered

Define

Axis variable (e.g. hospital)

Clustered variable (e.g. gender)

% of ca̲ses

OK

- To display this stacked bar chart as a compound histogram or clustered bar chart with the weighted data in Figure 6.1, first retrieve or re-create this file.
- Select 'Graphs' and then 'Bar', select 'Clustered' in the Bar Charts dialog box (Figure 2.12), which opens the 'Define Clustered Bar: Summaries for Groups of Cases' sub-dialog box (Figure 6.9).
- Select 'Hospitalisation(hospital)' and then the ▶ button beside the 'Category Axis:' text box, which puts 'Hospitalisation(hospital)' in this box (Figure 6.9).
- Select 'Gender(gender)' and then the ▶ button beside the 'Define Clusters by:' box, which puts 'Gender(gender)' in this box (Figure 6.9).
- Select '% of ca̲ses'.
- Select 'OK', which closes the 'Define Clustered Bar: Summaries for Groups of Cases' sub-dialog box and the Data Editor window and which displays the clustered bar chart shown in Figure 6.10 in the Viewer window.

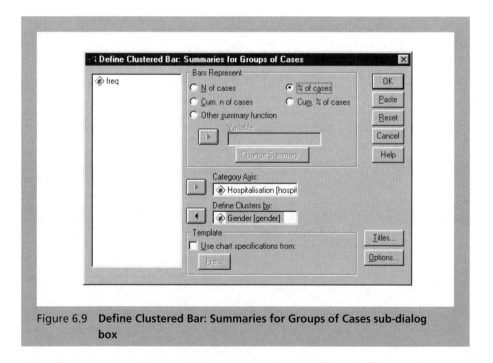

Figure 6.9　**Define Clustered Bar: Summaries for Groups of Cases sub-dialog box**

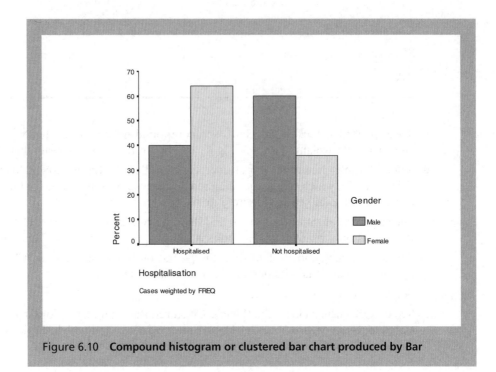

Figure 6.10   **Compound histogram or clustered bar chart produced by Bar**

Chapter 7

Correlation coefficients: Pearson's correlation and Spearman's rho

■ *There are a number of different correlation coefficients. The commonest by far is the Pearson Correlation Coefficient. It is a numerical measure or index of the amount of association between two sets of scores. It ranges in size from +1.00 through 0.00 to –1.00.*

■ *The '+' sign indicates a positive correlation – that is, the scores on one variable increase as the scores on the other variable increase. A '–' sign indicates a negative correlation – that is, as the scores on one variable increase, the scores on the other variable decrease.*

■ *A correlation of 1.00 indicates a perfect association between the two variables. In other words, a scattergram of the two variables will show that ALL of the points fit a straight line exactly. A value of 0.00 indicates that the points of the scattergram are essentially scattered randomly around any straight line drawn through the data or are arranged in a curvilinear manner. A correlation coefficient of –0.5 would indicate a moderate negative relationship between the two variables.*

■ *Spearman's rho is the Pearson Correlation Coefficient applied to the scores after they have been ranked from the smallest to the largest on the two variables separately. It is used when the basic assumptions of the Pearson Correlation Coefficient have not been met by the data – that is especially when the scores are markedly asymmetrical (skewed) on a variable.*

■ *Since correlation coefficients are usually based on samples of data, it is usual to include a statement of the statistical significance of the correlation coefficient. Statistical significance is a statement of the likelihood of obtaining a particular correlation coefficient for a sample of data IF there is no correlation (i.e. a correlation of 0.00) in the population from which the sample was drawn. SPSS can give statistical significance as an exact value or as one of the conventional critical significance levels (i.e. 0.05 and 0.01 for example).*

We will illustrate the computation of Pearson's correlation, a scatterdiagram and Spearman's rho for the data in Table 7.1 (*ISP* Table 7.1), which gives scores for the music ability and mathematical ability of 10 children. We begin by typing in the music scores in the first column of the Data Editor and the mathematics scores in the second column. Name the first column 'music', the second column 'maths' and remove the two zero decimal places as displayed in Figure 7.1. We then proceed to analyse the relationship between these two sets of scores.

Table 7.1   **Scores on musical ability and mathematical ability for 10 children**

Music score	Mathematics score
2	8
6	3
4	9
5	7
7	2
7	3
2	9
3	8
5	6
4	7

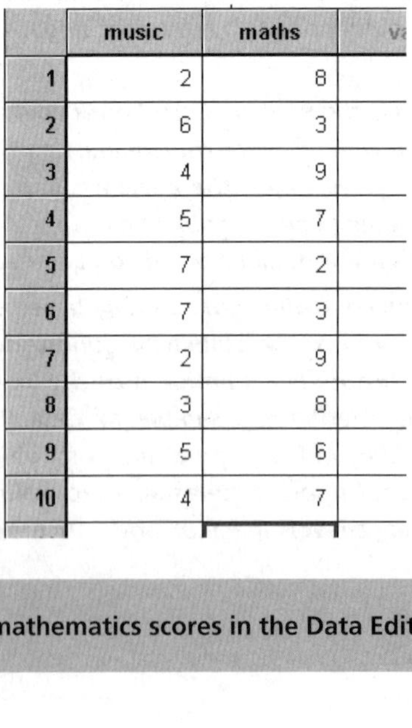

	music	maths	va
1	2	8	
2	6	3	
3	4	9	
4	5	7	
5	7	2	
6	7	3	
7	2	9	
8	3	8	
9	5	6	
10	4	7	

Figure 7.1   **Music and mathematics scores in the Data Editor**

7.1   Pearson's correlation

Quick summary

Analyze

Correlate

Bivariate

Select variables ▶

OK

- Select 'Analyze' from the menu bar towards the top of the window, which produces a drop-down menu (Figure 1.9).
- Select 'Correlate' from the drop-down menu, which reveals a smaller drop-down menu.
- Select 'Bivariate' from this drop-down menu, which opens the Bivariate Correlations dialog box (Figure 7.2).
- Select 'music' and 'maths' and then the ▶ button, which puts 'music' and 'maths' in the 'Variables:' text box. You can either select the two variables by

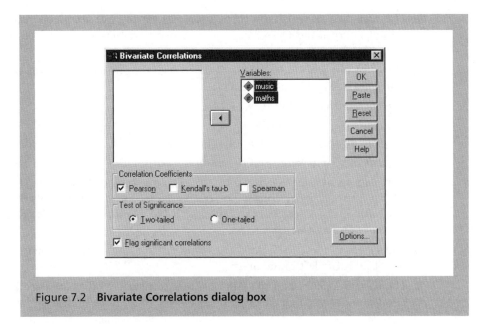

Figure 7.2   **Bivariate Correlations dialog box**

two separate operations or drag the highlight down over the second variable using the mouse. Click onto the highlight and move down to cover the second variable before releasing the mouse button.

■ The 'Pearson' option has already been pre-selected (i.e. it is a default option), so if only Pearson's correlation is required, select 'OK', which closes the Bivariate Correlations dialog box and the Data Editor window and which produces the output shown in Table 7.2 in the Viewer window.

Table 7.2   **Pearson's correlation produced by Correlate**

Correlations

		MUSIC	MATHS
MUSIC	Pearson Correlation	1	−.900**
	Sig. (2-tailed)	.	.000
	N	10	10
MATHS	Pearson Correlation	−.900**	1
	Sig. (2-tailed)	.000	.
	N	10	10

**Correlation is significant at the 0.01 level.

7.2   Interpreting the output in Table 7.2

■ The variables on which the correlation was carried out are given both in the columns and in the rows. We have just two variables so a 2×2 correlation matrix is generated.

■ The print-out gives indications of how to read the entries in the table [Pearson Correlation; Sig. (2-tailed); and N].

■ The correlation of MUSIC with MATHS is –0.900.

■ The exact significance level is given to three decimal places (.000). This is a very significant level. A two-tailed test of significance was requested.

■ 10 pairs of scores were used to obtain the correlation coefficient (10).

■ Correlations are displayed in a matrix. The diagonal of this matrix (from top left to bottom right) consists of the variable correlated with itself, which obviously gives a perfect correlation of 1. No significance level is given for this value as it never varies (.).

■ The values of the correlations are symmetrical around the diagonal from top right to bottom left in the matrix.

■ The computer has 'flagged' with the two asterisks (**) that the correlation is significant at the 0.01 (1%) significance level. With large matrices, this can be a useful aid to identifying significant relationships. This 'flagging' can be de-selected in the Bivariate Correlation dialog box.

7.3 Reporting the output in Table 7.2

■ The correlation between music ability and mathematical ability is –.900. It is usual to round correlations to two decimal places, which would make it –0.90. This is more than precise enough for most psychological measurements.

■ The exact significance level to three decimal places is .000. This means that the significance level is less than 0.001. We would suggest that you do not use a string of zeros, as these confuse people. Always change the third zero to a 1. This means means that the significance level can be reported as being $p < 0.001$.

■ It is customary to present the degrees of freedom (df) rather than the number of cases when presenting correlations. The degrees of freedom are the number of cases minus 2, which makes them 8 for this correlation. There is nothing wrong with reporting the number of cases instead.

■ In a report, we would write "There is a significant negative relationship between musical ability and mathematical ability ($r = –0.90, df = 8, p < 0.001$). Children with more musical ability have lower mathematical ability." Significance of the correlation coefficient is discussed in more detail in the textbook (*ISP*, Chapter 10).

7.4 Spearman's rho

Quick summary

Analyze

Correlate

Bivariate

Select Spearman and de-select Pearson

Select variables ▶

OK

To correlate the scores in ranks rather than as raw scores, one simply makes a different choice in the Bivariate Correlations dialog box:

■ To produce Spearman's correlation by itself, select 'Spearman' in the Bivariate Correlations dialog box shown in Figure 7.2 and de-select 'Pearson'.

■ Select 'OK', which closes the Bivariate Correlations dialog box and the Data Editor window and which produces the output shown in Table 7.3 in the Viewer window.

Table 7.3 **Spearman's correlation produced by Correlate**

Correlations

			MUSIC	MATHS
Spearman's rho	MUSIC	Correlation Coefficient	1.000	−.894**
		Sig. (2-tailed)	.	.000
		N	10	10
	MATHS	Correlation Coefficient	−.894**	1.000
		Sig. (2-tailed)	.000	.
		N	10	10

**Correlation is significant at the 0.01 level (2-tailed).

7.5   Interpreting the output in Table 7.3

■ The Spearman's instruction also prints out a matrix for two variables.

■ Spearman's correlation between the ranks for musical ability and mathematical ability is −.894.

■ The exact significance level is given to three decimal places as .000 but this is best handled by changing the final 0 to 1 (i.e. .001).

■ The number of cases on which that correlation was based is 10 and is given by N = 10 in the table.

■ The degrees of freedom are the number of cases minus 2, which makes them 8.

7.6   Reporting the output in Table 7.3

■ The correlation reported to two decimal places is −0.89.

■ The probability of achieving this correlation by chance is less than 0.001 (i.e. $p < 0.001$).

■ We would report this in the following way: "There is a statistically significant negative correlation between musical ability and mathematical ability (rho = −.89, $df = 8$, $p < 0.001$). Those with the highest musical ability tend to be those with the lowest mathematical ability and vice versa."

7.7   Scatter diagram

Quick summary

Graphs

Scatter

Put one variable into $\underline{X}$ Axis ▶ and another into the $\underline{Y}$ Axis ▶

OK

■ Select the 'Graphs' option on the menu bar towards the top of the window, which displays a drop-down menu (Figure 2.8).

■ Select 'Scatter . . .', which opens the Scatterplot dialog box (Figure 7.3).

■ Since the 'Simple' option is the default and so has already been pre-selected as indicated by the bold square frame surrounding it, select 'Define', which opens the Simple Scatterplot dialog box (Figure 7.4).

■ With a correlation it does not really matter which variable represents the horizontal or *x*-axis (the abscissa) and which variable the vertical or *y*-axis (the ordinate). We will specify the *y*-axis as being musical ability ('music') and the *x*-axis as being mathematical ability ('maths'), so select 'music' and the ▶ button beside the '$\underline{X}$ Axis:' box, which puts 'music' into this box as shown in Figure 7.4.

■ Select 'maths' and the ▶ button next to the '$\underline{Y}$ Axis:' box, which puts 'maths' into this box as shown in Figure 7.4.

■ Select 'OK', which closes the Simple Scatterplot dialog box and the Data Editor window and which displays the scatterdiagram shown in Figure 7.5 in the Viewer window.

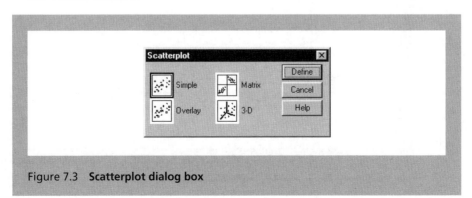

Figure 7.3   **Scatterplot dialog box**

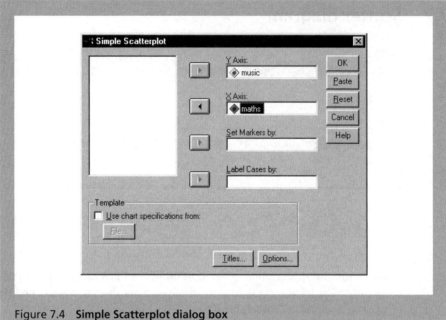

Figure 7.4   Simple Scatterplot dialog box

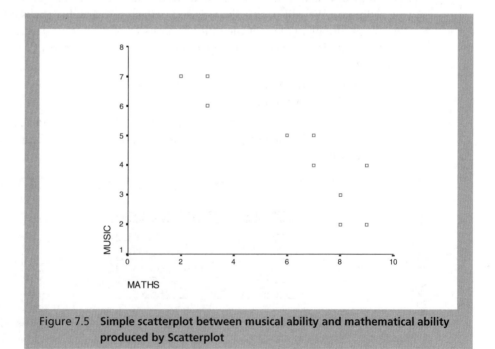

Figure 7.5   Simple scatterplot between musical ability and mathematical ability
produced by Scatterplot

7.8   Interpreting Figure 7.5

- ◼ The scatter of points is relatively narrow, indicating that the correlation is high.
- ◼ The slope of the scatter lies in a relatively straight line, indicating that it is a linear rather than a curvilinear relationship.
- ◼ If the relationship is curvilinear, then Pearson's or Spearman's correlation coefficients may be misleading.
- ◼ This line moves from the upper left to the lower right, which signifies a negative correlation.

7.9   Reporting Figure 7.5

- ◼ You should never report a correlation coefficient without examining the scattergram for problems such as curved relationships or outliers (*ISP*, Chapter 7).
- ◼ In a student project it should always be possible to include graphs of this sort. Unfortunately, journal articles and books tend to be restricted in the numbers they include because of economies of space and cost.
- ◼ We would write of Figure 7.5: "A scattergram of the relationship between mathematical ability and musical ability was examined. There was no evidence of a curvilinear relationship or the undue influence of outliers."

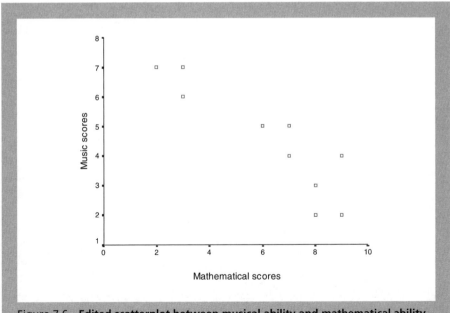

Figure 7.6   **Edited scatterplot between musical ability and mathematical ability produced by Scatterplot**

The bivariate correlations procedure allows you also to obtain Kendall's tau and one-tailed tests of significance. There is a variety of scatterplots available. These can be edited in many ways in the Chart Editor window by selecting Edit, SPSS Chart Object and Open. Explore these. Figure 7.6 shows some of the changes that can be achieved using the Chart Editor (see section 2.14).

Chapter 8

Regression: prediction with precision

- *If there is a relationship between two variables, it is possible to estimate or predict a person's score on one of the variables from their score on the other variable. The stronger the correlation, the better the prediction.*

- *Regression can be used on much the same data as the correlation coefficient. However, it is far less commonly used because of the problems of comparability between values obtained from different sets of variables.*

- *The simple regression technique described in this chapter expresses relationships in terms of the units of measurement of the variables involved. Thus if two different studies use slightly different variables it is difficult to compare the outcomes of the studies using this form of regression.*

- *The relationship between two variables in regression is expressed mathematically by the slope of the best fitting line through the points of the scattergram and the point at which this regression line cuts the (vertical) axis of the scattergram. In regression, therefore, the relationship between two variables requires a value of the slope (usually given the symbol 'B') and the intercept or cut-point in the vertical axis (usually given the symbol 'a').*

- *Regression becomes a much more important technique when one is using several variables to predict values on another variable. These techniques are known as multiple regression (see Chapters 28 and 29).*

We will illustrate the computation of simple regression and a regression plot with the data in Table 8.1 (*ISP* Table 7.1), which gives a score for the music ability and mathematical ability of 10 children. These data are identical to those used in the previous chapter on correlation. In this way, you may find it easier to appreciate the differences between regression and correlation. As shown in Figure 8.1, the music scores are in the first column of the Data Editor and the mathematics scores are in the second column.

The music scores ('music') are the criterion or the dependent variable while the mathematics scores ('maths') are the predictor or independent variable. With regression, it is essential to make the criterion or dependent variable the vertical axis (*y*-axis) of a scatterplot and the predictor or independent variable the horizontal axis (*x*-axis).

Table 8.1   Scores on musical ability and mathematical ability for
10 children

Music score	Mathematics score
2	8
6	3
4	9
5	7
7	2
7	3
2	9
3	8
5	6
4	7

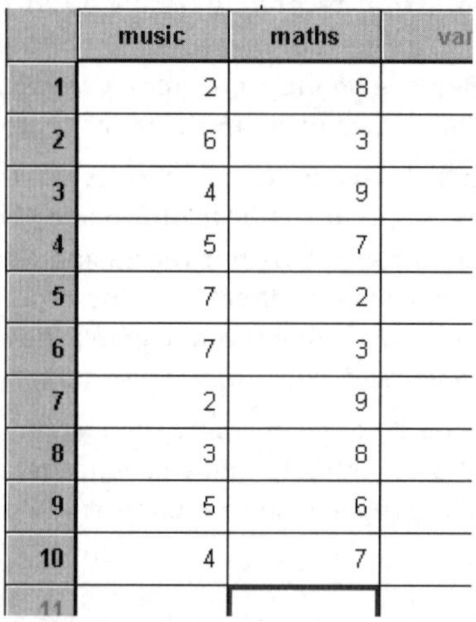

	music	maths	va
1	2	8	
2	6	3	
3	4	9	
4	5	7	
5	7	2	
6	7	3	
7	2	9	
8	3	8	
9	5	6	
10	4	7	
11			

Figure 8.1   Music and mathematics scores in the Data Editor

8.1   Simple regression equations

Quick summary

Analyze

Regression

Linear

Select ▶ *criterion/dependent variable for* Y *Axis*

Select ▶ *predictor/independent variable for* X *Axis*

OK

■ Select 'Statistics' from the menu bar towards the top of the window, which produces a drop-down menu (Figure 1.9).

■ Select 'Regression' from the drop-down menu, which reveals a smaller drop-down menu.

■ Select 'Linear . . .' from this drop-down menu, which opens the Linear Regression dialog box (Figure 8.2: Note this dialog box contains entries for the next two steps).

■ Select 'music' and then the ▶ button besides the 'Dependent:' box, which puts 'music' in this box.

■ Select 'maths' and then the ▶ button besides the 'Independent[s]:' box, which puts 'maths' in this box.

■ Select 'Statistics . . .', which opens the 'Linear Regression: Statistics' sub-dialog box (Figure 8.3).

■ Select 'Confidence intervals' and de-select 'Model fit'.

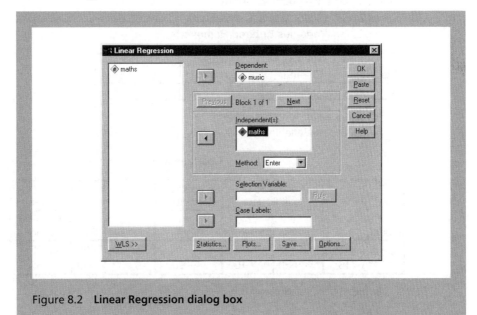

Figure 8.2 **Linear Regression dialog box**

■ Select 'Continue', which closes the 'Linear Regression: Statistics' sub-dialog box.

■ Select 'OK', which closes the Linear Regression dialog box and the Data Editor window and which produces the output shown in Table 8.2 in the Viewer window.

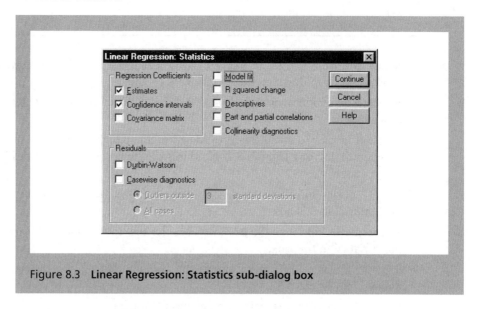

Figure 8.3   **Linear Regression: Statistics sub-dialog box**

Table 8.2   **Linear regression output**

Variables Entered/Removed[b]

Model	Variables Entered	Variables Removed	Method
1	MATHS[a]	.	Enter

a. All requested variables entered.
b. Dependent Variable: MUSIC.

Coefficients[a]

Model	Unstandardized Coefficients		Standardized Coefficients			95% Confidence Interval for B	
	B	Std. Error	Beta	t	Sig.	Lower Bound	Upper Bound
1 (Constant)	8.425	.725		11.620	.000	6.753	10.097
MATHS	−.633	.109	−.900	−5.832	.000	−.883	−.383

a. Dependent Variable: MUSIC.

8.2   Interpreting the output in Table 8.2

In simple regression involving two variables, it is conventional to report the regression equation as a slope (b) and an intercept (a) as explained in *ISP* (Chapter 8). SPSS does not quite follow this terminology but all of the relevant information is in Table 8.2. Unfortunately, at this stage the SPSS output is far more complex and detailed than the statistical sophistication of most students. The key basic elements of the output are highlighted in bold in the following list:

- **B is the slope. The slope of the regression line is called the *unstandardised regression coefficient* in SPSS. The unstandardised regression coefficient between 'music' and 'maths' is displayed under B and is –.633, which rounded to two decimal places is –0.63. What this means is that for every increase of 1.00 on the horizontal axis, the score on the vertical axis changes by –.633.**

- The 95% confidence interval for this coefficient ranges from –.88 (–.883) to –.38 (–.383). Since the regression is based on a sample and not the population, there is always a risk that the sample regression coefficient is not the same as that in the population. The 95% confidence interval gives the range of regression slopes within which you can be 95% sure that the population slope will lie.

- **The intercept (a) is referred to as the constant in SPSS. The intercept is presented as the (Constant) and is 8.425, which rounded to two decimal places is 8.43. It is the point at which the regression line cuts the vertical (Y) axis.**

- The 95% confidence interval for the intercept is 6.753 to 10.097. This means that, based on your sample, the intercept of the population is 95% likely to lie in the range of 6.75 to 10.10.

- The column headed 'Beta' gives a value of –.900. This is actually the Pearson correlation between the two variables. In other words, if you turn your scores into standard scores (z-scores) the slope of the regression and the correlation coefficient are the same thing.

8.3   Regression scatterplot

Quick summary

Graphs

Scatter . . .

Define

Select ▶ *criterion/dependent variable for Y Axis*

Select ▶ *predictor/independent variable for X Axis*

OK

Double click on scatterplot

Chart

Options . . .

Total

OK

It is generally advisable to inspect a scattergram of your two variables when doing regression. This involves the steps involved in plotting a scattergram as described in Chapter 7.

■ Select the 'Graphs' option on the menu bar near the top of the window, which displays a drop-down menu (Figure 2.8).

■ Select 'Scatter . . .', which opens the Scatter dialog box (Figure 7.3).

■ Since the Simple option is the default and so has already been pre-selected as indicated by the bold square frame surrounding it, select 'Define', which opens the Simple Scatterplot dialog box (Figure 7.4).

■ Select 'music' and the ▶ button next to the 'Y Axis:' box, which puts 'music' into this box as shown in Figure 7.4.

■ Select 'maths' and the ▶ button beside the 'X Axis:' box, which puts 'maths' into this box as shown in Figure 7.4.

■ Select 'OK', which closes the Simple Scatterplot dialog box and the Data Editor window and which displays the scatterdiagram shown in Figure 7.5 in the Viewer window.

To draw a regression line

■ Move the cursor into the scatterplot and double click on the left button of the mouse, which puts the scatterplot in the Chart Editor.

■ Select 'Chart' from the menu bar of the Chart Editor, which produces a drop-down menu (Figure 2.13).

■ Select 'Options . . .' from the Chart drop-down menu, which opens the Scatterplot Options dialog box (Figure 8.4).

■ Select 'Total' in the 'Fit Line' box.

■ Although not shown like this in the Chart Editor, the regression line in the scatterplot will be extended to intersect with the vertical axis in the Viewer window. Because the vertical line does not extend beyond 8, the regression line will not actually meet with the vertical line. To ensure that the regression line does intersect with the vertical line, it is necessary to extend the vertical

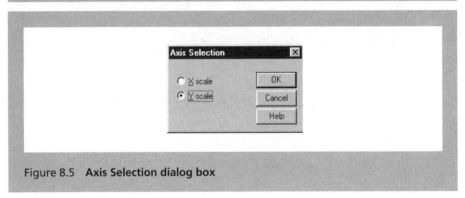

Figure 8.4   **Scatterplot Options sub-dialog box**

Figure 8.5   **Axis Selection dialog box**

line with the following procedure. Also the vertical axis does not extend to zero. This can be changed if necessary.

- Select 'Chart' on the menu bar of the Chart Editor window, which produces a drop-down menu (Figure 2.13).

- Select 'Axis . . .' on this menu, which opens the Axis Selection dialog box (Figure 8.5).

- Select the 'Y scale' (Figure 8.5).

- Select 'OK', which closes the Axis Selection dialog box and opens the 'Y Scale Axis' sub-dialog box (Figure 8.6).

- Highlight '1' in the text box beneath 'Minimum' in the Range section and type '0'.

- Highlight '8' in the text box beneath 'Maximum' in the Range section and type '9'.

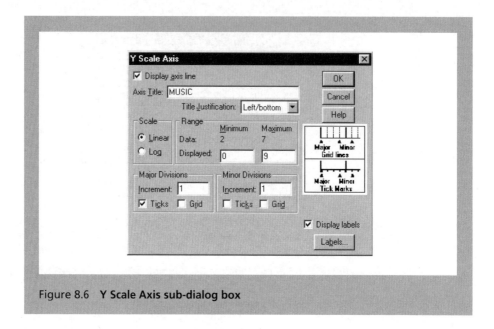

Figure 8.6   **Y Scale Axis sub-dialog box**

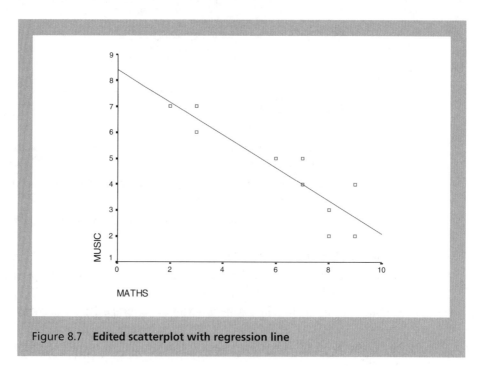

Figure 8.7   **Edited scatterplot with regression line**

■ Select 'OK', which closes the 'Y Scale Axis' sub-dialog box.

■ Figure 8.7 shows the scatterplot with the regression line extended to the vertical axis.

■ Select 'Close' which leaves the scatterplot in the Viewer window as shown in Figure 8.7.

■ The scale of the horizontal axis can be changed by selecting 'Y scale' in the Axis Selection dialog box (Figure 8.5) and 'OK', which opens the 'Y Scale Axis' sub-dialog box (Figure 8.6). In the box beside 'Increment:' in the 'Major Divisions' section you can change the '2' to '1'. In the box under 'Minimum' in the 'Range' section you can change the value to '0' if it is not already 0.

8.4   Interpreting Figure 8.7

This should be fairly obvious:

■ The regression line sloping from the top left down to bottom right indicates a negative relationship between the two variables. Remember that unless your axes intersect at zero on both the vertical and horizontal axes then your interpretation risks being mistaken.

■ The points seem relatively close to this line, which suggests that Beta (correlation) should be a large (negative) numerical value and that the confidence interval for the slope should be relatively small.

8.5   Reporting Table 8.2 and Figure 8.7

Although all of the output from SPSS is pertinent to a sophisticated user, many readers might prefer to have the bare bones at this stage.

■ With this in mind, we would write about the analysis in this chapter: "The scatterplot of the relationship between mathematical and musical ability suggested a linear negative relationship between the two variables. It is possible to predict accurately a person's musical ability from their mathematical ability. The equation is $Y' = 8.43 + (-0.63X)$ where X is an individual's mathematics score and Y' is the best prediction of their musical ability score."

■ An alternative is to give the scatterplot and to write underneath $a = 8.43$ and $B = -0.63$.

■ One could add the confidence intervals such as: "The 95% confidence interval for the slope of the regression line is $-.88$ to $-.38$. Since this confidence interval does not include 0.00 the slope differs significantly from a horizontal straight line." However, this would be a relatively sophisticated interpretation for novices in statistics.

Chapter 9

Samples and populations: generating a random sample

■ *Random sampling is a key aspect of statistics. This chapter explains how random samples can be quickly generated.*

■ *One can get a better 'feel' for inferential statistics and sampling by obtaining random samples from your data to explore the variability in outcomes of further statistical analyses on these random samples.*

■ *Random sampling can also be used with huge sets of data to carry out preliminary analyses. In the past, when computer time was expensive and computer processing slow, this would be of a great benefit.*

■ *Keep an eye on the dialog boxes as you work through this chapter. You will notice options which allow you to select samples based on other criteria such as the date when the participants were interviewed.*

In this chapter, the selection of random samples from a known set of scores is illustrated. The primary aim of this is to allow those learning statistics for the first time to try random sampling in order to get an understanding of sampling distributions. This should lead to a better appreciation of estimation in statistics and the frailty that may underlie seemingly hard-nosed mathematical procedures. We will illustrate the generation of a random sample from a set of data consisting of the extraversion scores of the 50 airline pilots shown in Table 4.1.

9.1 Selecting a random sample

Quick summary

Data

Select Cases . . .

Random sample of cases

Approximately

Enter % of sample

Continue

OK

■ As described in Chapter 1, type in the extraversion scores in the first column of the Data Editor or, if you have saved these data as a system file, call up this file.

■ Select 'Data' from the menu bar near the top of the window, which produces a drop-down menu (Figure 2.2).

■ Select 'Select Cases . . .' from this drop-down menu, which opens the Select Cases dialog box (Figure 9.1).

■ Select 'Random sample of cases' and then select 'Sample . . .', which opens the 'Select Cases: Random Sample' sub-dialog box (Figure 9.2).

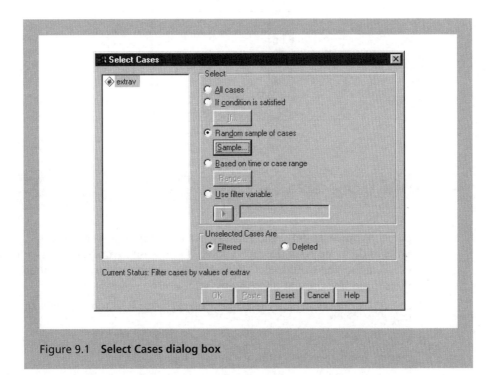

Figure 9.1   **Select Cases dialog box**

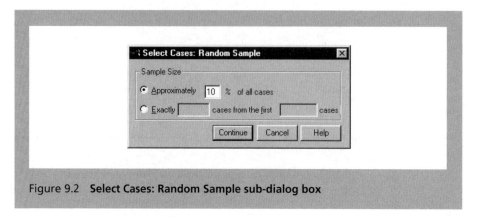

Figure 9.2   **Select Cases: Random Sample sub-dialog box**

	extrav	filter_$	var
1	3	0	
2	1	0	
3	4	0	
4	5	0	
5	3	0	
6	5	0	
7	2	0	
8	2	0	
9	3	1	
10	2	0	
11	5	0	

Figure 9.3   **Random selection of cases**

■ Select 'Approximately' and for, say, a 10% sample of 50 cases, type 10 in the box beside it and 50 in the second box. If you wanted an exact 10% of all cases (i.e. 5 cases) you would select 'Exactly', type '5' in the box beside it and '50' in the second box on that line (Figure 9.2).

■ Select 'Continue', which closes the 'Select Cases: Random Sample' sub-dialog box.

■ Select 'OK', which closes the Select Cases dialog box and, after a few moments, opens the Data Editor window (Figure 9.3).

9.2 Interpreting Figure 9.3

The second column is called 'filter_$' and consists of a series of 0s and 1s. The 1s represent the cases that have been selected and also do not have a line running through their row number indicating that they have been selected. Note that using this procedure in this instance (see Table 9.1) has resulted in seven cases being selected (i.e. 14%) and not five (i.e. 10%). If you selected another sample, the chances are that different individuals will have been selected and that the number of individuals may not be the same.

Table 9.1   **Descriptive statistics produced by Descriptives**

Descriptive Statistics

	N	Minimum	Maximum	Mean	Std. Deviation
EXTRAV	7	1	5	3.00	1.41
Valid N (listwise)					

9.3 Selecting the cases of the random sample

Quick summary

Data

Select Cases . . .

If condition is satisfied

filter_$

Continue

OK

■ Select 'Data' from the menu bar near the top of the window, which produces a drop-down menu (Figure 2.2).

■ Select 'Select Cases . . .' from this drop-down menu, which opens the Select Cases dialog box (Figure 9.1).

■ Select 'If condition is satisfied', which opens the 'Select Cases: If' sub-dialog box (Figure 9.4).

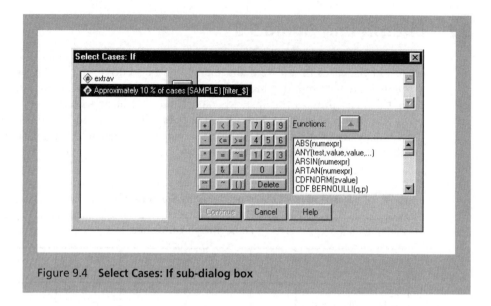

Figure 9.4   **Select Cases: If sub-dialog box**

■ Select 'Approximately 10% of cases (SAMPLE)(filter_$)' and then the ▶ button, which puts 'filter_$' in the box beside it.

■ Select 'Continue', which closes the 'Select Cases: If' sub-dialog box.

■ Select 'OK', which closes the Select Cases dialog box and returns to the Data Editor window. The random sample has now been selected.

9.4   Statistical analysis on random sample

Quick summary

Analyze

Descriptive Statistics

Descriptives . . .

variable (e.g. 'extrav')

▶

OK

■ Select 'Analyze' on the menu bar near the top of the window, which produces a drop-down menu (Figure 1.9).

- Select 'Descriptive Statistics' from the 'Analyze' drop-down menu, which displays a second drop-down menu (Figure 1.9).
- Select 'Descriptives . . .', which opens the Descriptives dialog box (Figure 1.10).
- Select 'extrav' and then the ▶ button, which puts 'extrav' in the 'Variable[s]:' text box.
- Select 'OK', which closes the Descriptives dialog box and the Data Editor window and which displays the output shown in Table 9.1 in the Viewer window.
- Remember that this random sample remains in force until you select 'Data' from the menu bar towards the top of the screen, 'Select Cases . . .' from the drop-down menu and 'All cases' from the Select Cases dialog box.

Chapter 10

Selecting cases

■ *This chapter explains how to select a particular subgroup from your sample. For example, you may wish to analyse the data only for young people or for women.*

Sometimes we may wish to carry out computations on subgroups in our sample. For example we may want to correlate musical and mathematical ability (a) in girls and boys separately, (b) in older and younger children separately and (c) in older and younger girls and boys separately. To do this, we need a code for sex and age such as 1 for girls and 2 for boys. We also need to decide what age we will use as a cutoff point to determine which children fall into the younger age group and which children fall into the older age group. We will use age 10 as the cutoff point, with children aged 9 or less falling into the younger age group and children aged 10 or more falling into the older age group. Then we need to select each of the groups in turn and carry out the computation. We will illustrate the selection of cases with the data in Table 10.1, which shows the music and mathematics scores of ten children together with their code for sex and their age

Table 10.1 **Scores on musical ability and mathematical ability for 10 children with their sex and age**

Music score	Mathematics score	Sex	Age
2	8	1	10
6	3	1	9
4	9	2	12
5	7	1	8
7	2	2	11
7	3	2	13
2	9	2	7
3	8	1	10
5	6	2	9
4	7	1	11

in years. (The music and mathematics scores are the same as those previously presented in Table 7.1.)

Obviously the selection of cutoff points is important. You need to beware of inadvertently excluding some cases.

10.1 Selecting cases

Quick summary

Data

Select Cases . . .

If condition is satisfied

If . . .

Selecting variable and ▶

Selecting condition (e.g. = 1)

Continue

OK

■ Enter the data in Table 10.1 in the Data Editor, putting music scores in the first column, mathematics scores in the second column, the code for sex in the third column and the age in years in the fourth column as shown in Figure 10.1. If you saved the music and mathematics scores for the data in Chapter 7, you can retrieve this data file and add in the code for sex and the age in years.

■ Select 'Data' from the menu bar near the top of the window, which produces a drop-down menu (Figure 2.2).

■ Select 'Select Cases . . .' from this drop-down menu, which opens the Select Cases dialog box (Figure 9.1).

■ Select 'If condition is satisfied'.

■ Select 'If . . .', which opens the 'Select Case: If' sub-dialog box (Figure 9.4).

■ *To select the girls*, select 'sex' and then the ▶ button, which puts 'sex' in the box beside it.

■ Select '=' button, which puts the '=' sign after 'sex'.

■ Select 1, which puts 1 after 'sex ='.

■ Select 'Continue', which closes the 'Select Case: If' sub-dialog box.

	music	maths	sex	age	va
1	2	8	1	10	
2	6	3	1	9	
3	4	9	2	12	
4	5	7	1	8	
5	7	2	2	11	
6	7	3	2	13	
7	2	9	2	7	
8	3	8	1	10	
9	5	6	2	9	
10	4	7	1	11	

Figure 10.1   Music and mathematics scores with sex and age in the Data Editor

■ Select 'OK', which closes the Select Cases dialog box and which returns to the Data Editor window. The fifth column is called 'filter_$'. The rows or cases selected have a 1 in this fifth column. Cases not selected have a 0 in them. Girls have now been selected.

■ Proceed with your statistical analysis (e.g. correlation).

■ *To select the boys* next, select 'Data' from the menu bar near the top of the window.

■ Select 'Select Cases . . .'.

■ Select 'If . . . sex = 1', which opens the 'Select Case: If' sub-dialog box.

■ Replace the '1' with a '2' so 'sex = 2'.

■ Select 'Continue', which closes the 'Select Case: If' sub-dialog box.

■ Select 'OK', which closes the Select Cases dialog box and returns to the Data Editor window. Boys have now been selected.

■ Proceed with your statistical analysis (e.g. correlation).

■ *To select the younger girls next*, that is the girls of 9 years and younger, select 'Data' from the menu bar near the top of the window.

■ Select 'Select Cases . . .'.

■ Select 'If . . . sex = 2', which opens the 'Select Case: If' sub-dialog box.

- Replace the '2' with a '1' so 'sex = 1'.
- Select '&'.
- Select 'age'.
- Select '<=' (less than or equal to).
- Select '9'.
- Select 'Continue', which closes the 'Select Case: If' sub-dialog box.
- Select 'OK', which closes the Select Cases dialog box and returns to the Data Editor window. Younger girls have now been selected.
- Proceed with your statistical analysis (e.g. correlation).

- *To select the older girls next*, that is the girls over 9 years, select Data from the menu bar near the top of the window.
- Select 'Select Cases . . .'.
- Select 'If . . . sex = 1 & age <= 9', which opens the 'Select Case: If' sub-dialog box.
- Replace '<=' with '>' (greater than).
- Select 'Continue', which closes the 'Select Case: If' sub-dialog box.
- Select 'OK', which closes the Select Cases dialog box and returns to the Data Editor window. Older girls have now been selected.
- Proceed with your statistical analysis (e.g. correlation).
- Remember that you need to select 'All cases' in the Select Cases dialog box if you wish to go back to analysing all of your cases.

Chapter 11

Standard error

■ *Standard error is an index of the standard deviation of the means of many samples taken from the population. In other words, it is a measure of the average amount by which the means of samples differ from the mean of the population from which they came.*

■ *It is generally most used as an intermediate step in other statistical techniques.*

■ *However, it can be used like variance or standard deviation as an index of the amount of variability in the scores on a variable.*

We will illustrate the computation of the estimated standard error of the mean with the set of six scores presented in Table 11.1 (*ISP* Table 11.3) which may represent self-esteem scores.

Table 11.1   **Data for standard error example**

Self-esteem scores
5
7
3
6
4
5

11.1 Estimated standard error of the mean

Quick summary

Enter data

Analyze

Descriptive Statistics

Descriptives . . .

variable

Options . . .

S. E. mean

Continue

OK

A number of SPSS procedures provide the standard error of the mean as part of the output.

■ As described in Chapter 1, enter the six scores in Table 11.1 in the first column of the Data Editor window.

■ Select 'Analyze' on the menu bar near the top of the window, which produces a drop-down menu (Figure 1.9).

■ Select 'Descriptive Statistics' from the Analyze drop-down menu, which displays a second drop-down menu (Figure 1.9).

■ Select 'Descriptives . . .', which opens the Descriptives dialog box (Figure 1.10).

■ Select 'var00001' and then the ▶ button, which puts 'var00001' in the 'Variable[s]:' text box.

■ Select 'Options . . .', which opens the 'Descriptives: Options' sub-dialog box (Figure 5.1).

■ Select 'S.E. mean'.

Table 11.2 **Standard error of the mean produced by Descriptives**

Descriptive Statistics

	N	Minimum	Maximum	Mean		Std.
	Statistic	Statistic	Statistic	Statistic	Std. Error	Statistic
ESTEEM	6	3	7	5.00	.58	1.41
Valid N (listwise)	6					

■ Select 'Continue', which closes the 'Descriptives: Define' sub-dialog box.

■ Select 'OK', which closes the Descriptives dialog box and the Data Editor window and which displays the output shown in Table 11.2 in the Viewer window.

11.2 Interpreting the output in Table 11.2

■ The table gives us the value of the standard error of sample means as 0.58, which is rounded to two decimal places. This is the 'average' amount by which means of samples (N = 6) differ from the population mean.

■ It is an estimate based on a sample and should really be termed the estimated standard error.

■ The table includes other information such as the mean (5.00), the estimated population standard deviation based on this sample, and the minimum and maximum values in the data.

■ The final column gives the (estimated) standard deviation of the six scores, which is 1.41.

11.3 Reporting the output in Table 11.2

Generally, in psychological statistics, one would not report the standard error of sample means on its own. It would be more usual to report it as part of certain tests of significance. However, in many circumstances it is just as informative as the variance or standard deviation of a sample, as it bears a simple relationship to both of these.

Chapter 12

The *t*-test: comparing two samples of correlated/related scores

■ *A common question in research is does the average (i.e. mean) score for one set of scores differ from the average score for another set of scores.*

■ *Because in research we invariably deal with samples of people drawn from the potential population in research, we need to estimate whether any difference we obtain between the two sets of scores is statistically significant. That is, is the obtained difference between the two means so very different from a zero difference that it is unlikely that the samples come from the same population.*

■ *There are two versions of the t-test. One is used when the two sets of scores to be compared come from a single set or sample of people or when the correlation coefficient between the two sets of scores is high. This is known as the related or correlated t-test. Turn to the next chapter if your two sets of scores come from two different groups of people.*

■ *(If you have used a matching procedure to make pairs of people similar on some other characteristics then you would also use the related t-test in the present chapter – especially if the two sets of scores correlate significantly).*

■ *Data entry for related and unrelated variables is very different in SPSS so take care to plan your analysis before entering your data in order to avoid problems and unnecessary work.*

■ *If you have more than two sets of scores to compare then turn to Chapter 21 on the related analysis of variance.*

We will illustrate the computation of a related *t*-test with the data in Table 12.1, which shows the number of eye-contacts made by the same babies with their mothers at 6 and 9 months (*ISP* Table 12.6).

Table 12.1   **Number of one-minute segments with eye-contact at different ages**

Baby	Six months	Nine months
Clara	3	7
Martin	5	6
Sally	5	3
Angie	4	8
Trevor	3	5
Sam	7	9
Bobby	8	7
Sid	7	9

12.1 Related *t*-test

Quick summary

Enter data

Analyze

Compare Means

Paired-Samples T Test . . .

var00001

var00002

OK

■ As described in Chapter 1, enter the data of Table 12.1 into the Data Editor, putting the number of eye-contacts at 6 months in the first column and the number of eye-contacts at 9 months in the second column (Figure 12.1). Label the variables and remove the two zero decimal places.

■ Save this data set, as it is used again in Chapter 18.

■ Select 'Analyze' on the menu bar near the top of the window, which produces a drop-down menu (Figure 1.9).

■ Select 'Compare Means' from this drop-down menu, which opens a second drop-down menu.

■ Select 'Paired-Samples T Test . . .', which opens the Paired-Samples T Test dialog box (Figure 12.2).

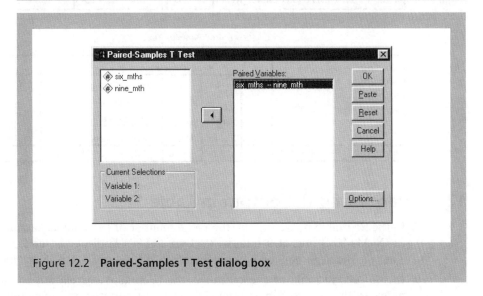

Figure 12.1   **Data Editor containing amount of eye-contact at two ages**

Figure 12.2   **Paired-Samples T Test dialog box**

■ Select 'six_mths', which puts it beside 'Variable 1:' in the Current Selections
section.

■ Select 'nine_mth', which puts it beside 'Variable 2:' in the Current Selections
section. Note that the variable that is ultimately put in as 'Variable 1:' has (1)
the shorter name and (2) alphabetical priority.

■ Select the ▶ button, which puts 'six_mths--nine_mth' in the 'Paired_Vari-
ables:' box.

■ Select 'OK', which closes the Paired-Samples T Test dialog box and the Data Editor window and which displays the output shown in Table 12.2 in the Viewer window.

Table 12.2 **Related *t*-test output**

Paired Samples Statistics

		Mean	N	Std. Deviation	Std. Error Mean
Pair 1	SIX_MTHS	5.25	8	1.91	.67
	NINE_MTH	6.75	8	2.05	.73

Paired Samples Correlations

	N	Correlation	Sig.
Pair 1 SIX_MTHS & NINE_MTH	8	.419	.301

Paired Samples Test

	Paired Differences							
				95% Confidence Interval of the Difference				Sig.
	Mean	Std. Deviation	Std. Error Mean	Lower	Upper	t	df	(2-tailed)
Pair 1 SIX_MTHS–NINE_MTH	−1.50	2.14	.76	−3.29	.29	−1.984	7	.088

12.2 Interpreting the output in Table 12.2

■ In the first table of the output, the mean number of eye-contacts at 6 months ('SIX_MTHS') and at 9 months ('NINE_MTH') is displayed under Mean. Thus the mean amount of eye contact is 5.25 at 6 months and 6.75 at 9 months.

■ In the second table of the output is the (Pearson) correlation coefficient between the two variables (eye-contact at six months and eye-contact at nine months). IDEALLY, the value of this should be sizeable (in fact it is .419) and statistically significant (which it is not with a 2-tail significance level of .301). The related *t*-test assumes that the two variables are correlated, and you might consider an unrelated *t*-test (Chapter 13) to be more suitable in this case.

■ In the third table of the output the difference between these two mean scores is presented under the 'Mean' of 'Paired Differences' and the standard error of this mean under 'Std. Error Mean'. The difference between the two means is –1.50 and the estimated standard error of means for this sample size is .76.

■ The *t*-value of the difference between the sample means, its degrees of freedom and its two-tailed significance level are also shown in this third table. The *t*-value is –1.984, which has an exact two-tailed significance level of .088 with 7 degrees of freedom.

12.3 Reporting the output in Table 12.2

■ We could report these results as follows: "The mean number of eye-contacts at 6 months (M = 5.25, SD = 1.91) and at 9 months (M = 6.75, SD = 2.05) did not differ significantly (*t* = –1.98, *df* = 7, two-tailed *p* = .088).".

■ In this book, to be consistent, we will report the exact probability level for non-significant results as above. However, it is equally acceptable to report them as '*p* > .05' or '*ns*' (which is short for non-significant).

■ Notice that the findings would have been statistically significant with a one-tailed test. However, this would have to have been predicted with sound reasons prior to being aware of the data. In this case one would have written to the effect "The two means differed significantly in the predicted direction (*t* = –1.98, *df* = 7, one-tailed *p* = .044).".

■ Once again, to be consistent throughout this book, we will report the exact probability level for significant findings where possible. Note that when SPSS displays the significance level as '.000', we need to present this as '*p* < .001' since the exact level is not given. It is equally acceptable to report significant probabilities as '*p* < .05', '*p* < .01' and '*p* < .001' as appropriate.

■ If you prefer to use confidence intervals, you could report your findings as: "The mean number of eye-contacts at 6 months was 5.25 (SD = 1.91) and at 9 months was 6.75 (SD = 2.05). The difference was 1.50. The 95% confidence interval for this difference is –3.29 to .29. Since the confidence interval passes through 0.00, the difference is not statistically significant at the two-tailed 5% level.".

■ The reporting of confidence intervals rather than significance levels is advocated by some statisticians. However, it remains relatively uncommon.

Chapter 13

The *t*-test: comparing two groups of unrelated/ uncorrelated scores

- *The uncorrelated or unrelated* t-test *is used to calculate whether the means of two sets of scores are significantly different from each other. It is the most commonly used version of the* t-test.

- *The unrelated* t-test *is used when the two sets of scores come from two different samples of people.*

- *(Turn to the previous chapter on the related* t-test *if your scores come from just one set of people or if you have employed a matching procedure.)*

- *Data entry for related and unrelated variables is very different in SPSS so take care to plan your analysis before entering your data in order to avoid problems and unnecessary work.*

- *SPSS procedures for the unrelated* t-test *are very useful since they include an option for its calculation when the variances of the two samples of scores are significantly different from each other. This is very rarely mentioned in statistics textbooks but is valuable nonetheless. If you have more than two sets of scores to compare, then turn to Chapter 20 on the unrelated analysis of variance.*

We will illustrate the computation of an unrelated *t*-test with the data in Table 13.1 which shows the emotionality scores of 12 children from two-parent families and 10 children from single-parent families (*ISP* Table 13.8). In SPSS this sort of *t*-test is called an independent samples *t*-test.

Table 13.1   **Emotionality scores in two-parent and lone-parent families**

Two-parent family X_1	Lone-parent family X_2
12	6
18	9
14	4
10	13
19	14
8	9
15	8
11	12
10	11
13	9
15	
16	

13.1 Unrelated *t*-test

Quick summary

Enter data

Var00001 contains code for the two groups

Var00002 consists of the dependent variable

Analyze

Compare Means

Independent-Samples T Test . . .

Grouping variable (e.g. var00001)

Define Groups . . .

1

2

Continue

Dependent or test variable (e.g. var00002)

OK

	family	emotion
1	2	12
2	2	18
3	2	14
4	2	10
5	2	19
6	2	8
7	2	15
8	2	11
9	2	10
10	2	13
11	2	15
12	2	16
13	1	6
14	1	9

Figure 13.1   **Data Editor containing the code for unrelated groups in 'family' and the scores of the dependent variable in 'emotion' for 14 cases**

■ Take a good look at Figure 13.1. Notice that there are two columns of data. The second column ('emotion') consists of the 22 emotionality scores from BOTH groups of children. The data are not kept separate for the two groups. In order to identify to which group the child belongs, the first column ('family') contains lots of 1s and 2s. These indicate, in our example, children from a lone-parent family (they are the rows with 1s in 'family') and children from two-parent families (they are the rows with 2s in 'family'). Thus a single column is used for the dependent variable (in this case, emotionality, 'emotion') and another column for the independent variable (in this case, type of family, 'family'). So each row is a particular child, and their independent variable and dependent variable scores are entered in two separate columns in the Data Editor.

■ Save this data set, as it is used again in Chapter 18.

■ Select 'Analyze' on the menu bar near the top of the window, which produces a drop-down menu (Figure 1.9).

- Select 'Compare Means' from this drop-down menu, which opens a second drop-down menu.
- Select 'Independent-Samples T Test . . .', which opens the Independent-Samples T Test dialog box (Figure 13.2).
- Select 'family' and the ▶ button beside 'Grouping Variable:', which puts 'family' in this box.
- Select Define Groups . . .', which opens the 'Define Groups' sub-dialog box (Figure 13.3).
- Type '1' in the box beside 'Group 1:'.
- Select box beside 'Group 2:' and type '2'.
- Select 'Continue', which closes the 'Define Groups' sub-dialog box.

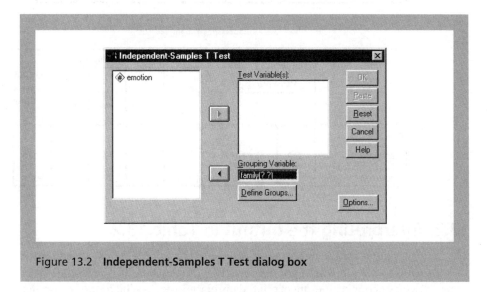

Figure 13.2   **Independent-Samples T Test dialog box**

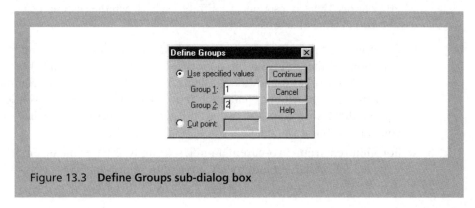

Figure 13.3   **Define Groups sub-dialog box**

- Select 'emotion' and the ▶ button beside 'Test Variable[s]:', which puts 'emotion' in this box.
- Select 'OK', which closes the Independent-Samples T Test dialog box and the Data Editor window and which displays the output shown in Table 13.2.

Table 13.2   Unrelated *t*-test output

Group Statistics

	FAMILY	N	Mean	Std. Deviation	Std. Error Mean
EMOTION	1	10	9.50	3.10	.98
	2	12	13.42	3.37	.97

Independent Samples Test

	Levene's Test for Equality of Variances		t-test for Equality of Means					95% Confidence Interval of the Difference	
	F	Sig.	t	df	Sig. (2-tailed)	Mean Differ-ence	Std. Error Differ-ence	Lower	Upper
EMOTION Equal variances assumed	.212	.650	−2.813	20	.011	−3.92	1.39	−6.82	−1.01
Equal variances not assumed			−2.836	19.768	.010	−3.92	1.38	−6.80	−1.03

13.2 Interpreting the output in Table 13.2

The output for the uncorrelated/unrelated *t*-test on SPSS is particularly confusing even to people with a good knowledge of statistics. The reason is that there are two versions of the uncorrelated/unrelated *t*-test. Which one to use depends on whether or not there is a significant difference between the (estimated) variances for the two groups of scores.

- Examine the first table of the output. This contains the means and standard deviations of the scores on the dependent variable (emotionality) of the two groups. Notice that an additional figure has been added by the computer to the name of the column containing the dependent variable. This additional figure indicates which of the two groups the row refers to. If you had labelled your values, these value labels would be given in the table.

- For children from two-parent families ('family 2') the mean emotionality score is 13.42 and the standard deviation of the emotionality scores is 3.37. For the children of lone-parent families ('family 1') the mean emotionality score is 9.50 and the standard deviation of emotionality is 3.10.

■ In the second table, read the line 'Levene's Test for Equality of Variances'. If the probability value is statistically significant then your variances are UNEQUAL. Otherwise they are regarded as equal.

■ Levene's test for equality of variances in this case tells us that the variances are equal because the *p* value of .650 is not statistically significant.

■ Consequently, you need the row for 'Equal variances assumed'. The *t* value, its degrees of freedom and its probability are displayed. The *t* value for equal variances is –2.813, which with 20 degrees of freedom has an exact two-tailed significance level of .011.

■ Had Levene's test for equality of variances been statistically significant (i.e. .05 or less), then you should have used the second row of the output which gives the *t*-test values for unequal variances.

13.3 Reporting the results of Table 13.2

■ We could report the results of this analysis as follows: "The mean emotionality scores of children from two-parent families (M = 13.42, SD = 3.37) is significantly higher ($t = -2.81$, $df = 20$, two-tailed $p = .011$) than that of children in lone-parent families (M = 9.50, SD = 3.10).".

■ It is unusual to see the *t*-test for unequal variances in psychological reports. Many psychologists are unaware of its existence. So what happens if you have to use one? In order to clarify things, we would write: "Because the variances for the two groups were significantly unequal ($F = 8.43$, $p < .05$), a *t*-test for unequal variances was used . . .".

■ If you prefer to use the confidence intervals in Table 13.2, you might write: "The difference between the emotionality scores for the children from two-parent families (M = 13.42, SD = 3.37) and lone-parent families (M = 9.50, SD = 3.10) is –3.92. The 95% confidence interval for this difference is –6.82 to –1.01. Since this interval does not include 0.00, the difference is statistically significant at the two-tailed 5% level.".

Chapter 14

Chi-square: differences between samples of frequency data

■ Chi-square is generally used to assess whether two or more samples each consisting of frequency data (nominal data) differ significantly from each other. However, it can also be used to test whether a single sample differs significantly from a known population. The latter application is the least common because population characteristics are rarely known in research.

■ It is essential to remember that Chi-square requires frequencies, and PERCENTAGES SHOULD NEVER BE ENTERED, as they will give misleading outcomes.

■ Also remember that data for Chi-square analysis need to include the data from every individual only once. That is, the total frequencies should be the same as the number of people used in the analysis.

■ The analysis and interpretation of 2×2 contingency tables is straightforward. However, interpretation of larger contingency tables is not quite so easy and may require the table to be broken down into a number of smaller tables. Partitioning Chi-square, as this is known, usually requires adjustment to the significance levels to take into account the number of sub-analyses carried out. Consult a statistics textbook for more details.

■ This chapter also includes the Fisher-exact test, which can be useful in some circumstances when the assumptions of the Chi-square are not met by your data (especially when the expected frequencies are too low).

■ Also included is the McNemar test for significance of changes, which is closely related to Chi-square.

We will illustrate the computation of Chi-square with two or more samples with the data in Table 14.1 (*ISP* Table 14.8). This table shows which one of three types of television programme is favoured by a sample of 119 teenage boys and girls. To analyse a table of data like this one with SPSS we first have to input the data into the Data Editor and weight the cells by the frequencies of cases in them.

Table 14.1   **Relationship between favourite TV programme and sex**

Respondents	Soap opera	Crime drama	Neither
Males	27	14	19
Females	17	33	9

As we are working with a ready-made table, it is necessary to go through the 'Weighting Cases' procedure first (see Figure 14.1). Otherwise, you would enter the above table case by case, indicating which category of the row and which category of the column each case belongs to (see Figure 14.2).

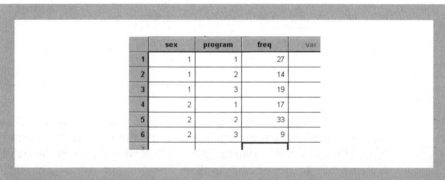

Figure 14.1   **Weighted cases in the Data Editor**

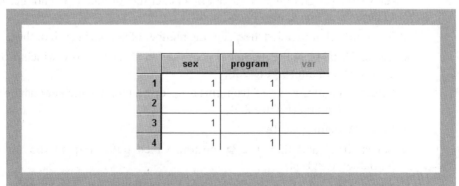

Figure 14.2   **Unweighted cases in the Data Editor**

14.1 Weighting data

(Ignore this section if you are not using a ready-made table)

Quick summary

Enter code for rows in first column

Enter code for columns in second column

Enter frequencies in third column

Data

Weight Cases . . .

Weight cases by

third variable (e.g. 'freq')

▶

OK

- We need to identify each of the six cells in Table 14.1. The rows of the table represent the sex of the participants, while the columns represent the three types of television programme. We will then weight each of the six cells of the table by the number of cases in them.
- The first column, called 'sex' in Figure 14.1, contains the code for males (1) and females (2). (These values have also been labelled.)
- The second column, called 'program', holds the code for the three types of television programme: soap opera (1); crime drama (2); and neither (3). (These values have also been labelled.)
- The third column, called 'freq', has the number of people in each of these six cells.
- Select 'Data' from the menu bar near the top of the window, which produces a drop-down menu (Figure 2.2).
- Select 'Weight Cases . . .' from this drop-down menu, which opens the Weight Cases dialog box (Figure 2.3).
- Select 'Weight cases by'.
- Select 'freq' and then the ▶ button, which puts 'freq' in the 'Frequency Variable:' text box.
- Select 'OK', which closes the Weight Cases dialog box. The six cells are now weighted by the numbers in the third column.

14.2 Chi-square for two or more samples

In this chapter we have concentrated on how one can analyse data from pre-existing contingency tables. This is why we need the weighting procedure. However, you will not always be using ready-made tables. Any variables which consist of just a small number of nominal categories can be used for Chi-square. For example, if one wished to examine the relationship between sex (coded 1 for male, 2 for female) and age (coded 1 for under 20 years, 2 for 20 to 39 years, and 3 for 40 years and over), the procedure is as follows. (a) Enter the age codes for your, say, 60 cases in the first column of the Data Editor. (b) Enter the age categories for each of these cases in the equivalent row of the next column. You can then carry out your Chi-square as follows. You do not go through the weighting procedure first. The frequencies in the cells are calculated by the computer for you.

Quick summary

Analyze

Descriptive Statistics

Crosstabs . . .

row variable (e.g. sex)

▶ *Row[s]:*

column variable (e.g. program)

▶ *Column[s]:*

Statistics . . .

Chi-square

Continue

Cells . . .

Expected

Unstandardized

Continue

OK

■ Select 'Analyze' on the menu bar near the top of the window, which produces a drop-down menu (Figure 1.9).

■ Select 'Descriptive Statistics' from the 'Statistics' drop-down menu, which displays a second drop-down menu (Figure 1.9).

■ Select 'Crosstabs . . .', which opens the Crosstabs dialog box (Figure 14.3).

■ Select 'sex' and then the ▶ button beside 'Row[s]:', which puts 'sex' in this box.

■ Select 'program' and then the ▶ button beside 'Column[s]:', which puts 'program' in this box.

■ Select 'Statistics . . .', which opens the 'Crosstabs: Statistics' sub-dialog box (Figure 14.4).

■ Select 'Chi-square'.

■ Select 'Continue', which closes the 'Crosstabs: Statistics' sub-dialog box.

■ Select 'Cells . . .', which opens the 'Crosstabs: Cell Display' sub-dialog box (Figure 14.5).

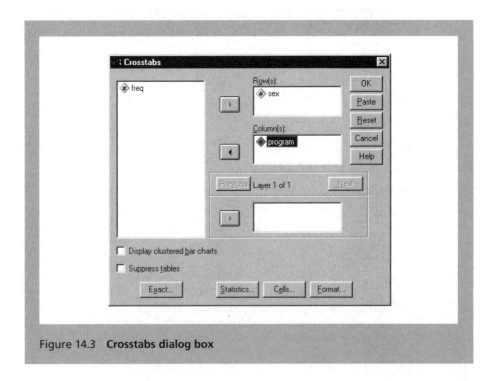

Figure 14.3   **Crosstabs dialog box**

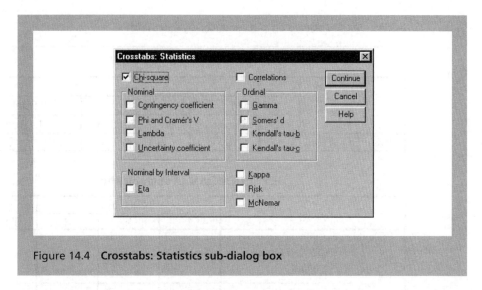

Figure 14.4   **Crosstabs: Statistics sub-dialog box**

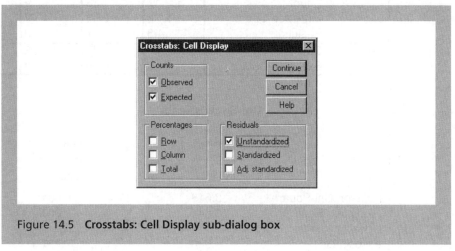

Figure 14.5   **Crosstabs: Cell Display sub-dialog box**

■ Select 'Expected' in the Counts section.

■ Select 'Unstandardized' in the 'Residuals' section.

■ Select 'Continue', which closes the 'Crosstabs: Cell Display' sub-dialog box.

■ Select 'OK', which closes the Crosstabs dialog box and the Data Editor window and which displays the output shown in Table 14.2 in the Viewer window.

Table 14.2   **Chi-square output produced by Crosstabs**

Case Processing Summary

	Cases					
	Valid		Missing		Total	
	N	Percent	N	Percent	N	Percent
SEX* PROGRAM	119	100.0%	0	.0%	119	100.0%

SEX* PROGRAM Crosstabulation

		PROGRAM			Total
		1	2	3	
SEX 1	Count	27	14	19	60
	Expected Count	22.2	23.7	14.1	60.0
	Residual	4.8	−9.7	4.9	
2	Count	17	33	9	59
	Expected Count	21.8	23.3	13.9	59.0
	Residual	−4.8	9.7	−4.9	
Total	Count	44	47	28	119
	Expected Count	44.0	47.0	28.0	119.0

Chi-Square Tests

	Value	df	Asymp. Sig. (2-sided)
Pearson Chi-Square	13.518a	2	.001
Likelihood Ratio	13.841	2	.001
Linear-by-Linear Association	.000	1	.987
N of Valid Cases	119		

a. 0 cells (.0%) have expected count less than 5. The minimum expected count is 13.88.

14.3 Interpreting the output in Table 14.2

■ The second (middle) table shows the observed and expected frequencies of cases and the difference (residual) between them for each cell. The observed frequency (called Count) is presented first and the expected frequency (called Expected Count) second. The observed frequencies are always whole numbers, so they should be easy to spot. The expected frequencies are always expressed to one decimal place, so they are easily identified. Thus the first cell of the table (males liking soap opera) has an observed frequency of 27 and an expected frequency of 22.2.

■ The final column in this table (labelled 'Total') lists the number of cases in that row followed by the expected number of cases in the table. So the first row has 60 cases, which will always be the same as the expected number of cases (i.e. 60.0).

■ Similarly, the final row in this table (labelled 'Total') first presents the number of cases in that column followed by the expected number of cases in the table for that column. Thus the first column has 44 cases, which will always be equal to the expected number of cases (i.e. 44.0).

■ **The Chi-square value, its degrees of freedom and its significance level are displayed in the third table on the line starting with the word Pearson, the man who developed this test. The Chi-square value is 13.518 which, rounded to two decimal places, is 13.52. Its degrees of freedom are 2 and its exact two-tailed probability is .001.**

■ Also shown underneath this table is the 'minimum expected count' of any cell in the table, which is 13.88 for the last cell (females liking neither). If the minimum expected frequency is less than 5.0 then we should be wary of using Chi-square. If you have a 2 × 2 Chi-square and small expected frequencies occur, it would be better to use the Fisher exact test which SPSS prints in the output in these circumstances.

14.4 Reporting the output in Table 14.2

There are two alternative ways of describing these results. To the inexperienced eye they may seem very different but they amount to the same thing:

■ We could describe the results in the following way: "There was a significant difference between the observed and expected frequency of teenage boys and girls in their preference for the three types of television programme (χ^2 = 13.51, df = 2, p = .001).".

■ Alternatively, and just as accurate: "There was a significant association between sex and preference for different types of television programme (χ^2 = 13.51, df = 2, p = .001).".

■ In addition, we need to report the direction of the results. One way of doing this is to state that: "Girls were more likely than boys to prefer crime programmes and less likely to prefer soap operas or both programmes.".

14.5 Fisher's exact test

The Chi-square procedure computes Fisher's exact test for 2 × 2 tables when one or more of the four cells has an expected frequency of less than 5. Fisher's exact test would be computed for the data in Table 14.3 (*ISP* Table 14.14).

Table 14.3 **Photographic memory and sex**

	Photographic memory	No photographic memory
Males	2	7
Females	4	1

The SPSS output for this table is presented in Table 14.4.

Table 14.4 **Fisher's exact test probabilities produced by Crosstabs for 2 × 2 table with expected frequencies of less than 5**

Case Processing Summary

	Cases					
	Valid		Missing		Total	
	N	Percent	N	Percent	N	Percent
SEXª MEMORY	14	100.0%	0	.0%	14	100.0%

SEX* MEMORY Crosstabulation

			MEMORY		
			Photographic	Non-photographic	Total
SEX Males	Count		2	7	9
	Expected Count		3.9	5.1	9.0
Females	Count		4	1	5
	Expected Count		2.1	2.9	5.0
Total	Count		6	8	14
	Expected Count		6.0	8.0	14.0

Chi-Square Tests

	Value	df	Asymp. Sig. (2-sided)	Exact Sig. (2-sided)	Exact Sig. (1-sided)
Pearson Chi-Square	4.381[b]	1	.036		
Continuity Correction[a]	2.340	1	.126		
Likelihood Ratio	4.583	1	.032		
Fisher's Exact Test				.091	.063
Linear-by-Linear Association	4.069	1	0.044		
N of Valid Cases	14				

a. Computed only for a 2 × 2 table.

b. 3 cells (75.0%) have expected count less than 5. The minimum expected count is 2.14.

14.6 Interpreting the output in Table 14.4

The significance of Fisher's exact test for this table is .091 at the two-tailed level and .063 at the one-tailed level.

14.7 Reporting the output in Table 14.4

■ We would write: "There was no significant relationship between sex and the possession of a photographic memory (two-tailed Fisher exact $p = .091$)." or "Males and females do not differ in the frequency of possession of a photographic memory (two-tailed Fisher exact $p = .091$)."

■ However, with such a small sample size, the finding might best be regarded as marginally significant and a strong recommendation made that further studies should be carried out in order to establish with more certainty whether girls actually do possess photographic memories more frequently.

14.8 One-sample Chi-square

Quick summary

Enter code for categories in first column (e.g. 'category') of Data Editor

Enter frequency of cases in second column (e.g. 'freq')

Data

Weight Cases . . .

Weight cases by

second variable (e.g 'freq')

OK

Analyze

Nonparametric Tests

Chi-square . . .

first variable (e.g. 'category')

Values:

Type expected value

Add

Repeat as needed

OK

We will illustrate the computation of a one-sample Chi-square with the data in Table 14.5 (*ISP* Table 14.16), which shows the observed and expected frequency of smiling in 80 babies. The expected frequencies were obtained from an earlier large-scale study.

Table 14.5   **Data for a one-sample Chi-square**

	Clear smilers	Clear non-smilers	Impossible to classify
Observed frequency	35	40	5
Expected frequency	40	32	8

- In the first column, labelled 'category', of the Data Editor enter the code for the three categories of smilers as shown in Figure 14.6.
- In the second column, labelled 'freq', enter the observed frequency of babies falling in the three categories.
- Weight the three categories as described at the beginning of this chapter (section 14.1).
- Select 'Analyze' on the menu bar near the top of the window, which produces a drop-down menu (Figure 1.9).

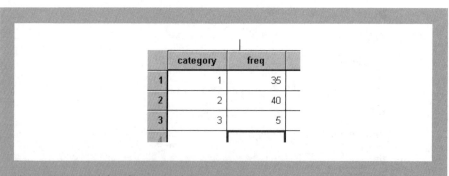

Figure 14.6   **Weighted cases in three categories**

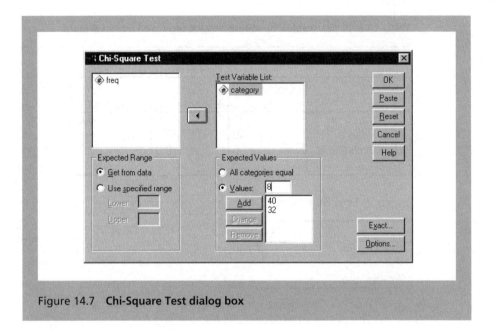

Figure 14.7   **Chi-Square Test dialog box**

- ■ Select 'Nonparametric Tests' from this drop-down menu, which opens a second drop-down menu.
- ■ Select 'Chi-square . . .', which opens the Chi-Square Test dialog box (Figure 14.7).
- ■ Select 'category' and then the ▶ button, which puts 'category' in the 'Test Variable List:' box.
- ■ Select 'Values:' in the Expected Values section.
- ■ Type '40' in the 'Values:' box.
- ■ Select 'Add'.
- ■ Type '32' in the 'Values:' box.
- ■ Select 'Add'.
- ■ Type '8' in the 'Values:' box.
- ■ Select 'Add'.
- ■ Select 'OK', which closes the Chi-Square Test dialog box and the Data Editor window and which displays the output shown in Table 14.6 in the Viewer window.

Table 14.6   **One-sample Chi-square output produced by Chi-Square**

CATEGORY

	Observed N	Expected N	Residual
Smilers	35	40.0	−5.0
Non-smilers	40	32.0	8.0
Unclassifiable	5	8.0	−3.0
Total	80		

Test Statistics

	CATEGORY
Chi-Square[a]	3.750
df	2
Asymp. Sig.	.153

a. 0 cells (.0%) have expected frequencies less than 5.
The minimum expected cell frequency is 8.0.

14.9 Interpreting the output in Table 14.6

■ The labels of the three categories are shown in the first column of the first table.

■ The observed frequencies of cases are presented in the second column under the heading of 'Observed N'.

■ The expected frequencies of cases are displayed in the third column under the heading of 'Expected N'.

■ The differences or residuals between the observed and expected frequencies are listed in the fourth column under the heading of 'Residual'.

■ The value of Chi-square, its degrees of freedom and its significance are presented in the second table. Chi-square, rounded to two decimal places, is 3.75, its degrees of freedom are 2 and its exact significance level is .153.

14.10 Reporting the output in Table 14.6

We could describe the results of this analysis as follows: "There was no statistical difference between the observed and expected frequency for the three categories of smiling in infants ($\chi^2 = 3.75$, $df = 2$, $p = .153$).".

14.11 McNemar test

We will illustrate the computation of McNemar's test with the data in Table 14.7, which shows the number of teenage children who changed or did not change their minds about going to university after listening to a careers talk favouring university education (*ISP* Table 14.17). The table gives the numbers who wanted to go to university before the talk and after it (30), those who wanted to go before the talk but not after it (10), those who wanted to go to university after the talk but not before it (50), and the numbers not wanting to go to university both before and after the talk (32).

Table 14.7   **Students wanting to go to university before and after a careers talk**

	1 Before talk 'yes'	**2 Before talk 'no'**
1 After talk 'yes'	30	50
2 After talk 'no'	10	32

Quick summary

Enter code for rows in first column ('after') of table

Enter code for columns in second column ('before') of table

Enter frequencies in third column ('freq') of table

Data

Weight Cases . . .

Weight cases by

'freq'

OK

Analyze

Nonparametric Tests

2 Related Samples . . .

row variable (e.g. 'after')

column variable (e.g. 'before')

Wilcoxon

McNemar

OK

■ In the first column (labelled 'after') of the Data Editor enter the code for the two columns representing the 'after the talk' position as shown in Figure 14.8.

■ In the second column (labelled 'before') enter the code for the two columns representing the 'before the talk' position.

■ In the third column (labelled 'freq') enter the observed frequency of teenagers falling into the four cells of the table.

■ Remove the two zero decimal places for the three variables. Note that the labels of the two values of the first two variables (say 1 for 'Yes' and 2 for 'No') do not appear in the output.

■ Weight the four cells as described at the beginning of this chapter (section 14.1).

■ Select 'Analyze' on the menu bar near the top of the window, which produces a drop-down menu (Figure 1.9).

■ Select 'Nonparametric Tests' from this drop-down menu, which opens a second drop-down menu.

■ Select '2 Related Samples . . .', which opens the Two-Related-Samples Tests dialog box (Figure 14.9).

	after	before	freq
1	1	1	30
2	1	2	50
3	2	1	10
4	2	2	32
5			

Figure 14.8   **Weighted cells for a McNemar test**

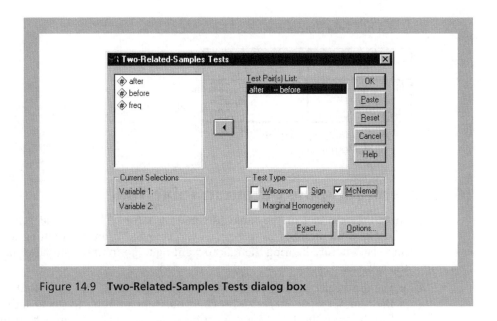

Figure 14.9   **Two-Related-Samples Tests dialog box**

- Select 'after', which puts it next to 'Variable 1:' in the Current Selections section.
- Select 'before', which puts it next to 'Variable 1:' in the Current Selections section. Note that the variable that is ultimately put in as 'Variable 1:' has (1) the shorter name and (2) alphabetical priority. Select the ▶ button, which puts 'after-before' in the 'Test Pair[s] List:' box.
- Select 'Wilcoxon' in the Test Type section to de-activate it.
- Select 'McNemar'.
- Select 'OK', which closes the Two-Related-Samples Tests dialog box and the Data Editor window and which displays the output shown in Table 14.8 in the Viewer window.

Table 14.8   **McNemar test output produced by 2 Related Samples**

AFTER & BEFORE

AFTER	BEFORE	
	1	2
1	30	50
2	10	32

Test Statisticsb

	AFTER & BEFORE
N	122
Chi-Squarea	25.350
Asymp. Sig.	.000

a. Continuity Corrected.
b. McNemar Test.

14.12 Interpreting the output in Table 14.8

■ In the second cell of the table (defined by 1 for 'AFTER' and 2 for 'BE-FORE') is the number of teenagers who changed from not wanting to go to university before hearing the talk to wanting to go to university after hearing the talk (i.e. 50).

■ In the third cell of the table (defined by 2 for 'AFTER' and 1 for 'BEFORE') is the number of teenagers who changed from wanting to go to university before hearing the talk to not wanting to go to university after hearing the talk.

■ The Chi-square value, rounded to two decimal places, is 25.350 and its significance level is less than .0005.

14.13 Reporting the output in Table 14.8

We can report the results of this analysis as follows: "There was a significant increase in the number of teenagers who wanted to go to university after hearing the talk ($\chi^2 = 25.35$, $df = 1$, $p < .001$).".

Chapter 15

Missing values

- ■ *Sometimes in research, you may not have a complete set of data from each participant. Missing values tells the computer how to deal with such situations.*

- ■ *Missing values can also be used to instruct the computer to ignore cases with a particular value(s) on particular variables.*

15.1 Introduction

When collecting data, information for some of the cases on some of the variables may be missing. Take, for example, the data in Table 15.1, which consists of the music and mathematics scores of 10 children with their code for gender and their age in years. There is no missing information for any of the four variables for any of the 10 cases. But suppose that the first two cases were away for the music test so that we had no scores for them. It would be a pity to discard all the data for these two cases because we have information on them for the other three variables of mathematics, gender and age. Consequently we would enter the data for these other variables. Although we could leave the music score cells empty for these two cases, what we usually do is to code missing data with a number which does not correspond to a possible value that the variable could take. Suppose the scores for the music test can vary from 0 to 10. We can use any number, other than 0 to 10, to signify a missing value for the music test. We will use the number 11 as the code for a missing music score so that the values in the first two rows of the first column are 11. We will also assume that the age for the third case is missing. We will use the number 0 as the code for age which is missing. Now we need to tell SPSS how we have coded missing data. If we do not do this, then SPSS will read these codes as real numbers.

Missing values can also be used to tell the computer to ignore certain values of a variable which you wish to exclude from your analysis. So, for example, you could use missing values in relation to Chi-square to get certain categories ignored.

Leaving a cell blank in the Data Editor spreadsheet results in a full stop (.) being entered in the cell if it is part of the active matrix of entries. On the output these are identified as missing values but they are best regarded as omitted

Table 15.1   **Scores on musical ability and mathematical ability for 10 children with their sex and age**

Music score	Mathematics score	Sex	Age
2	8	1	10
6	3	1	9
4	9	2	12
5	7	1	8
7	2	2	11
7	3	2	13
2	9	2	7
3	8	1	10
5	6	2	9
4	7	1	11

values. We would recommend that you do not use blank cells as a way of identifying missing values since this does not distinguish between truly missing values and keyboard errors. Normally, substantial numbers such as 99 or 999 are the best way of identifying a missing value.

15.2 Defining missing values

Quick summary

Variable View in Data Editor

Missing column cell

. . .

Code

Continue

OK

■ Enter the data in Table 15.1 in the Data Editor, including the missing values for the music test and age. If you saved the data used in Chapter 10, then you can retrieve these data.

3:age 0

	music	maths	sex	age
1	11	8	1	10
2	11	3	1	9
3	4	9	2	0
4	5	7	1	8
5	7	2	2	11
6	7	3	2	13
7	2	9	2	7
8	3	8	1	10
9	5	6	2	9
10	4	7	1	11

Figure 15.1 **Music and mathematics scores with sex and age in the Data Editor**

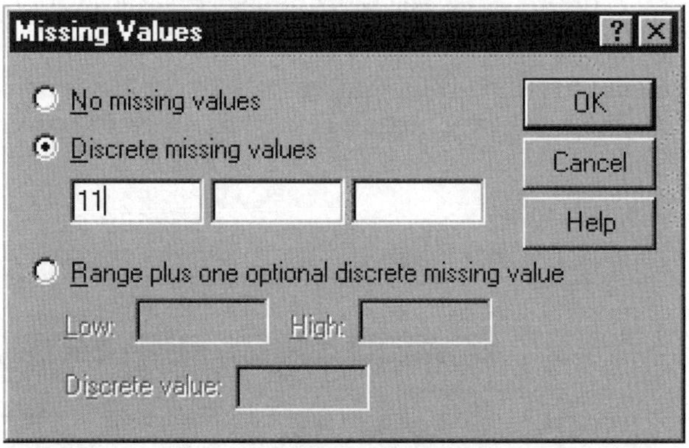

Figure 15.2 **Missing Values dialog box**

- To code missing values for a variable, select the 'Variable View' window in the Data Editor.
- Select the appropriate cell in the 'Missing' column which produces three dots called an ellipse.

- Select the ellipse which opens the Missing Values dialog box (Figure 15.2).

- Select 'Discrete missing values' and type '11' in the first box.

- Select 'OK' which closes the Missing Values dialog box.

- Repeat the procedure for the fourth column typing '0' in the first box.

15.3 Pairwise and listwise options

We will illustrate some of the options available when you have missing data with the Correlate procedure, although similar kinds of options are available with some of the other statistical procedures.

- Select 'Analyze', which produces a drop-down menu (Figure 1.9).

- Select 'Correlate' from the drop-down menu, which reveals a smaller drop-down menu.

- Select 'Bivariate' from this drop-down menu, which opens the Bivariate Correlations dialog box (Figure 7.2).

- Select 'music', 'maths', 'sex' and 'age' and then the ▶ button, which puts these variables in the 'Variables:' text box.

- Select 'Options . . .', which opens the 'Bivariate Correlations: Options' sub-dialog box (Figure 15.3).

- The default missing values option is 'Exclude cases pairwise'. This means that a correlation will be computed for all cases which have non-missing values for

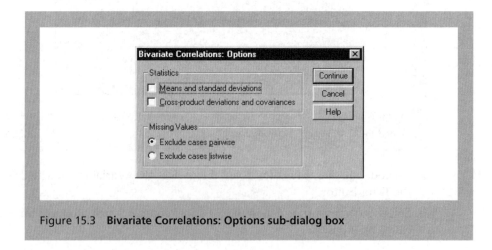

Figure 15.3   **Bivariate Correlations: Options sub-dialog box**

any pair of variables. Since there are two missing values for the music test and no missing values for the mathematics test and gender, the number of cases on which these correlations will be based is 8 as shown in Table 15.2. Since one value for age is missing for another case, the number of cases on which the correlation between music scores and gender is based is 7. As there are no missing values for the mathematics test and gender, the number of cases on which this correlation is based is 10. Finally, the number of cases on which the correlation between the mathematics score and age is 9 since there is one missing value for age and none for mathematics.

■ NOTICE THAT THE NUMBER OF CASES VARIES FOR PAIRWISE DELETION OF MISSING VALUES.

Table 15.2 **Exclude cases pairwise output for Correlate**

Correlations

		MUSIC	MATHS	SEX	AGE
MUSIC	Pearson Correlation	1.000	−.923**	.293	.681
	Sig. (2-tailed)	.	.001	.482	.092
	N	8	8	8	7
MATHS	Pearson Correlation	−.923**	1.000	−.161	−.550
	Sig. (2-tailed)	.001	.	.656	.125
	N	8	10	10	9
SEX	Pearson Correlation	.293	−.161	1.000	.118
	Sig. (2-tailed)	.482	.656	.	.762
	N	8	10	10	9
AGE	Pearson Correlation	.681	−.550	.118	1.000
	Sig. (2-tailed)	.092	.125	.762	.
	N	7	9	9	9

** Correlation is significant at the 0.01 level (2-tailed).

■ The alternative missing values option is 'Exclude cases listwise' in which correlations are computed for all cases which have no missing values on the variables which have been selected for this procedure. In this example, the number of cases which have no missing values on any of the four variables selected is 7 as shown in Table 15.3, which presents the output for this option.

■ NOTICE THAT THE NUMBER OF CASES DOES NOT VARY IN LIST-WISE DELETION OF MISSING VALUES.

Table 15.3   **Exclude cases listwise output for Correlate**

Correlations[a]

		MUSIC	MATHS	SEX	AGE
MUSIC	Pearson Correlation	1.000	−.956**	.354	.681
	Sig. (2-tailed)	.	.001	.437	.092
MATHS	Pearson Correlation	−.956**	1.000	−.483	−.729
	Sig. (2-tailed)	.001	.	.272	.063
SEX	Pearson Correlation	.354	−.483	1.000	.088
	Sig. (2-tailed)	.437	.272	.	.852
AGE	Pearson Correlation	.681	−.729	.088	1.000
	Sig. (2-tailed)	.092	.063	.852	.

** Correlation is significant at the 0.01 level (2-tailed).
a Listwise N=7.

15.4 Interpreting the output in Tables 15.2 and 15.3

There is little in the output which has not been discussed in other chapters. The only thing to bear in mind is that the statistics are based on a reduced number of cases.

15.5 Reporting the output in Tables 15.2 and 15.3

Remember to report the actual sample sizes (or degrees of freedom) used in reporting each statistical analysis rather than the number of cases overall.

Chapter 16

Recoding values

- *From time to time researchers need to alter how certain values of a variable are recorded by the computer; perhaps several different values need to be combined into one.*

- *The recoding values procedure allows you considerable flexibility to quickly and easily modify how any value has been coded numerically.*

16.1 Introduction

Sometimes we need to recode values for a particular variable in our data. There can be many reasons for this, including:

1. To put together several categories of a nominal variable which otherwise has very few cases. This is commonly employed in statistics such as Chi-square.

2. To place score variables into ranges of scores.

3. To recode items needing to be scored in the reverse way (see Chapter 17).

We may wish to categorise our sample into two or more groups according to some variable such as age or intelligence. We will illustrate the recoding of cases with the data in Table 16.1, which shows the music and mathematics scores of 10 children together with their code for gender and their age in years. The music and mathematics scores are the same as those previously presented in Table 7.1. Suppose that we wanted to compute the correlation between the music and mathematics scores for the younger and older children. To do this, we would first have to decide how many age groups we wanted. Since we have only 10 children we will settle for two groups. Next we decide what the cutoff point in age will be for the two groups. As we want two groups of similar size, we will select 10 as the cutoff point with children younger than 10 falling into one group and children aged 10 or more into the other group. We will now use SPSS to recode age in this way.

Table 16.1   **Scores on musical ability and mathematical ability for 10 children with their sex and age**

Music score	Mathematics score	Sex	Age
2	8	1	10
6	3	1	9
4	9	2	12
5	7	1	8
7	2	2	11
7	3	2	13
2	9	2	7
3	8	1	10
5	6	2	9
4	7	1	11

16.2 Recoding values

Quick summary

Enter data in Data Editor

Transform

Recode

Into Different Variables . . .

Variable to be recoded and ▶

Name: box

Type name of recoded variable

Change

Old and New Values . . .

   Old value or range of old values

   Type old value

   Value: box

   Type new value

   Add

   Repeat as necessary

Continue

OK

- Enter the data in Table 16.1 in the Data Editor, putting music scores in the first column, mathematics scores in the second column, the code for gender in the third column and the age in years in the fourth column as shown in Figure 16.1. If you saved the data used in Chapter 10, then you can retrieve this data file.

- Select 'Transform' from the menu bar near the top of the window, which produces a drop-down menu (Figure 16.2).

- Select 'Recode', which produces a second drop-down menu (Figure 16.2).

- Select 'Into Different Variables . . .', which opens the Recode into Different Variables dialog box (Figure 16.3) and which creates a separate variable for you to store the recoded values. This is useful when you do not wish to lose the original values as in this case.

- Select 'age' and the ▶ button, which puts 'age' in the box called 'Numeric Variable –> Output Variable:'.

- Select box under 'Name:' and type in name for the recoded variable (e.g. 'agecat').

- Select 'Change'.

- Select 'Old and New Values . . .', which opens the 'Recode into Different Variables: Old and New Values' sub-dialog box (Figure 16.4).

- Select 'Range:' in the Old Value section and type '9' in the box beside 'Lowest through'.

	music	maths	sex	age
1	2	8	1	10
2	6	3	1	9
3	4	9	2	12
4	5	7	1	8
5	7	2	2	11
6	7	3	2	13
7	2	9	2	7
8	3	8	1	10
9	5	6	2	9
10	4	7	1	11

Figure 16.1 **Music and mathematics scores with sex and age in the Data Editor**

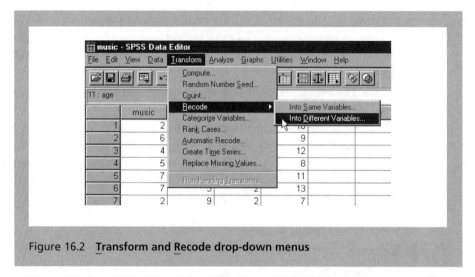

Figure 16.2   **Transform and Recode drop-down menus**

Figure 16.3   **Recode into Different Variables dialog box**

■ Select the box beside 'Value:' in the New Value section and type '1'.

■ Select 'Add', which puts 'Lowest thru 9 –> 1' in the 'Old –> New:' box.

■ Select 'Range:' and type '10' in the box beside 'through highest'.

■ Select the box beside 'Value:' in the New Value section and type '2'.

■ Select 'Add', which puts '10 thru Highest –> 2' in the 'Old –> New:' box.

■ Select 'Continue', which closes the 'Recode into Different Variables: Old and New Values' sub-dialog box.

■ Select 'OK', which closes the Recode into Different Variables dialog box and which inserts the recoded values for age in the fifth column of the Data Editor called 'agecat' as shown in Figure 16.5.

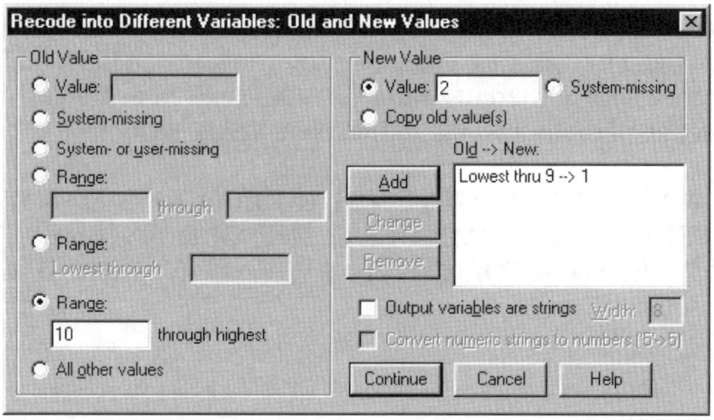

Figure 16.4   **Recode into Different Variables: Old and New Values sub-dialog box**

	music	maths	sex	age	agecat
1	2	8	1	10	2.00
2	6	3	1	9	1.00
3	4	9	2	12	2.00
4	5	7	1	8	1.00
5	7	2	2	11	2.00
6	7	3	2	13	2.00
7	2	9	2	7	1.00
8	3	8	1	10	2.00
9	5	6	2	9	1.00
10	4	7	1	11	2.00

Figure 16.5   **Age recoded as categories ('agecat') in the Data Editor**

16.3 Reporting the output

With a complex set of data it is very easy to forget precisely what you have done to your data. Recoding can radically alter the output from a computer analysis. You need to carefully check the implications of any recodes before reporting them.

16.4 Recoding missing values

Note that if there are missing values (as for 'age' in Figure 15.1) it is necessary to code these by selecting 'System- or user-missing' in the 'Old Value' section of the 'Recode into Different Variables: Old and New Values' sub-dialog box and selecting 'System-missing' in the 'New Value' section.

ALWAYS CHECK THAT YOUR RECODING HAS WORKED AS YOU INTENDED BY COMPARING THE OLD AND NEW VALUES IN THE DATA EDITOR FOR EACH NEW VALUE FOR ONE OR MORE CASES.

Chapter 17

Computing new variables

■ *Computing new variables allows you to add, subtract, etc. scores on several variables to give you a new variable. For example, you might wish to add together several questions on a questionnaire to give an overall index of what the questionnaire is measuring.*

17.1 Introduction

When analysing data we may want to form a new variable out of one or more old ones. For example, when measuring psychological variables, several questions are often used to measure more or less the same thing. For instance, the following four statements might be used to assess satisfaction with life:

a. I generally enjoy life

b. Some days things just seem to get me down

c. Life often seems pretty dull

d. The future looks hopeful.

Participants are asked to state how much they agree with each of these statements on the following four-point scale:

> 1: Strongly agree   2: Agree   3: Disagree   4: Strongly disagree

We may use these four items to determine how satisfied people are with their lives by adding up their responses to all four of them.

Notice a problem that frequently occurs when dealing with questionnaires: if you answer 'Strongly agree' to the first and fourth items you indicate that you enjoy life, whereas if you answer 'Strongly agree' to the second and third items you imply that you are dissatisfied with life. We want higher scores to denote greater life satisfaction. Consequently, we will reverse the scoring for the *first* and *fourth* items as follows:

> 1: Strongly disagree   2: Disagree   3: Agree   4: Strongly agree

We can use the 'Recode' procedure described in Chapter 16 to recode the values for the first and fourth items.

The data in Table 17.1 show the answers to the four statements by three individuals, and the way in which the answers to the first and fourth items have to be recoded. We will use these data to illustrate the SPSS procedure for adding together the answers to the four statements to form an index of life satisfaction.

Table 17.1   Life satisfaction scores of three respondents

	(a) Enjoy life (recode)	(b) Get me down (no recode)	(c) Dull (no recode)	(d) Hopeful (recode)
Respondent 1	Agree (2 recoded as 3)	Agree (2)	St. disagree (4)	Agree (2 recoded as 3)
Respondent 2	Disagree (3 recoded as 2)	Disagree (3)	Agree (2)	St. disagree (4 recoded as 1)
Respondent 3	St. agree (1 recoded as 4)	Disagree (3)	Disagree (3)	Disagree (3 recoded as 2)

17.2 Computing a new variable

Quick summary

Transform

Compute . . .

Name of new variable

Formula for new variable

OK

■ Enter the data in Table 17.1 in the Data Editor as shown in Figure 17.1.
■ Select 'Transform' from the menu bar near the top of the window, which produces a drop-down menu (Figure 16.2).
■ Select 'Compute . . .', which opens the Compute Variable dialog box (Figure 17.2).
■ Type the name of the new variable (e.g. 'lifesat') in the 'Target Variable:' box.
■ Select 'q1' and the ▶ button, which puts 'q1' in the 'Numeric Expression:' box.
■ Select '+' which puts '+' in the 'Numeric Expression:' box.

	q1	q2	q3	q4	
1	3	2	4	3	
2	2	3	2	1	
3	4	3	3	2	

Figure 17.1 **Coded answers to four items in the Data Editor**

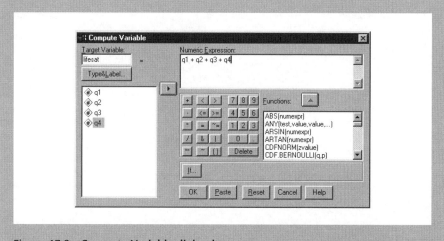

Figure 17.2 **Compute Variable dialog box**

3:lifesat		12			
	q1	q2	q3	q4	lifesat
1	3	2	4	3	12.00
2	2	3	2	1	8.00
3	4	3	3	2	12.00

Figure 17.3 **Computed new variable in the Data Editor**

■ Repeat the above two steps for 'q2', 'q3' and 'q4' so that 'lifesat = q1+q2+q3+q4' as shown in Figure 17.2.

■ Select 'OK', which closes the Compute Variable dialog box and returns to the Data Editor window displaying the new variable and its values as shown in Figure 17.3.

CHECK THAT THE VALUES FOR THE NEW VARIABLE ARE WHAT THEY SHOULD BE.

Do not forget to save your newly computed variables along with the rest of the spreadsheet Data Editor on exiting SPSS if you are likely to want to use them again.

Chapter 18

Ranking tests: non-parametric statistics

■ Sometimes you may wish to know whether the 'means' of two different sets of scores are significantly different from each other but feel that the requirement that the scores on each variable are roughly normally distributed (bell-shaped) is not fulfilled. Non-parametric tests can be used in these circumstances.

■ (Strictly speaking, non-parametric statistics do not test for differences in means. They cannot, since they use scores turned into ranks. Usually they test whether the ranks in one group are typically larger or smaller than the ranks in the other groups.)

■ We have included the Sign test and Wilcoxon's test for related data.

■ The Mann–Whitney U test is used for unrelated data.

We will illustrate the computation of two non-parametric tests for related scores with the data in Table 18.1, which was also used in Chapter 12 and which shows the number of eye-contacts made by the same babies with their mothers at six and nine months. Notice that the Sign test (section 18.1) and the Wilcoxon Matched Pairs test (section 18.4) produce different significance levels. The Sign test seems rather less powerful at detecting differences than the Wilcoxon Matched Pairs test.

Table 18.1   Number of one-minute segments with eye-contact at different ages

Baby	Six months	Nine months
Clara	3	7
Martin	5	6
Sally	5	3
Angie	4	8
Trevor	3	5
Sam	7	9
Bobby	8	7
Sid	7	9

18.1 Related scores: Sign test

Quick summary

Retrieve/enter data

Analyze

Nonparametric Tests

2 Related Samples . . .

var00001

var00002

Wilcoxon

Sign

OK

■ If you saved the data set used in Chapter 12, retrieve it. Otherwise create it again.

■ Select 'Analyze' on the menu bar near the top of the window, which produces the drop-down menu (Figure 1.9).

■ Select 'Nonparametric Tests' from this drop-down menu, which opens a second drop-down menu.

■ Select '2 Related Samples . . .', which opens the Two-Related-Samples Tests dialog box shown in Figure 18.1.

■ Select 'six_mths', which puts it besides 'Variable 1:' in the Current Selections section.

■ Select 'nine_mth', which puts it besides 'Variable 2:' in the Current Selections section. Note that the variable that is ultimately put in as 'Variable 1:' has (1) the shorter name and (2) alphabetical priority.

■ Select the ▶ button, which puts 'six_mths--nine_mth' in the 'Test Pair[s] List:' box.

■ (If you wish) select Wilcoxon to de-select it.

■ Select 'Sign'.

■ Select 'OK', which closes the Two-Related-Samples Test dialog box and the Data Editor window and which displays the output shown in Table 18.2 in the Viewer window.

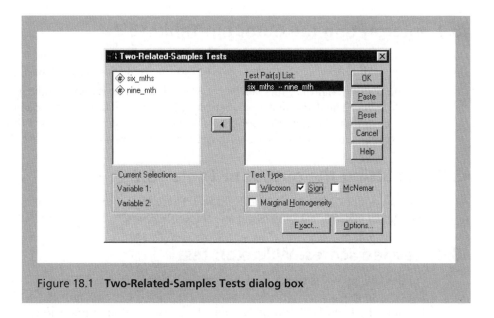

Figure 18.1 **Two-Related-Samples Tests dialog box**

Table 18.2 **Sign test output**

Frequencies

			N
NINE_MTH–SIX_MTHS	Negative Differences[a]		2
	Positive Differences[b]		6
	Ties[c]		0
	Total		8

a. NINE_MTH < SIX_MTHS.
b. NINE_MTH > SIX_MTHS.
c. SIX_MTHS = NINE_MTH.

Test Statistics[b]

	NINE_MTH - SIX_MTHS
Exact Sig. (2-tailed)	.289[a]

a. Binomial distribution used.
b. Sign Test.

18.2 Interpreting the output in Table 18.2

■ This is straightforward. There are 2 negative signed differences and 6 positive signed differences. There were no ties, so the number of cases is 8.

■ The two-tailed probability is .289 or 29%, which is clearly not significant at the 5% level. The Binomial distribution refers to the statistical technique by which probabilities can be found for samples consisting of just two different possible values, as is the case with the Sign test (given that we ignore ties).

18.3 Reporting the output in Table 18.2

We could report these results as follows: "There was no significant change in the amount of eye-contact between 6 and 9 months (Sign test, $N = 8$, $p = .289$).".

18.4 Related scores: Wilcoxon test

As the 'Wilcoxon' is the default option on the Two-Related-Samples Tests dialog box, simply select 'OK', which closes the Two-Related-Samples Tests dialog box and the Data Editor window and which displays the output shown in Table 18.3 in the Viewer window.

Table 18.3   **Wilcoxon test output**

Ranks

		N	Mean Rank	Sum of Ranks
NINE_MTH–SIX_MTHS	Negative Ranks	2a	3.00	6.00
	Positive Ranks	6b	5.00	30.00
	Ties	0c		
	Total	8		

a. NINE_MTH < SIX_MTHS.
b. NINE_MTH > SIX_MTHS.
c. SIX_MTHS = NINE_MTH.

Test Statisticsb

	NINE_MTH - SIX_MTHS
Z	–1.706a
Asymp. Sig. (2-tailed)	.088

a. Based on negative ranks.
b. Wilcoxon Signed Ranks Test.

18.5 Interpreting the output in Table 18.3

■ The output tells us that there are two cases which were negatively signed after ranking and six cases which were positively signed after ranking. It seems clear that 'NINE_MTH' tends to have larger values than 'SIX_MTHS'.

■ Instead of using tables of critical values, the computer uses a formula which relates to the z distribution. The z value is -1.706, which has a two-tailed probability of .088. This means that the difference between the two variables is not statistically significant at the 5% level.

18.6 Reporting the output in Table 18.3

We could report these results as follows: "There was no significant difference in the amount of eye-contact by babies between 6 and 9 months (Wilcoxon, $N = 8$, $z = -1.71$, two-tailed $p = .088$).".

18.7 Unrelated scores: Mann–Whitney U test

We will illustrate the computation of one non-parametric test for unrelated scores with the data in Table 18.4, which shows the emotionality scores of 12 children from two-parent families and 10 children from single-parent families.

Table 18.4 Emotionality scores in two-parent and lone-parent families

Two-parent family X_1	Lone-parent family X_2
12	6
18	9
14	4
10	13
19	14
8	9
15	8
11	12
10	11
13	9
15	
16	

Quick summary

Retrieve/enter data

Analyze

Nonparametric Tests

2 Independent Samples . . .

Dependent or test variable (e.g. 'emotion')

▶

Grouping variable (e.g. 'family')

▶

Define Groups . . .

1

2

Continue

OK

- If you saved the data set used in Chapter 13, retrieve it. Otherwise create it again.
- Select 'Analyze' on the menu bar near the top of the window, which produces the drop-down menu (Figure 1.9).
- Select 'Nonparametric Tests' from this drop-down menu, which opens a second drop-down menu.
- Select '2 Independent Samples . . .', which opens the Two-Independent-Samples Tests dialog box shown in Figure 18.2.
- Select 'emotion' and the ▶ button beside 'Test Variable List:', which puts 'emotion' in this box.
- Select 'family' and the ▶ button beside 'Grouping Variable:', which puts 'family' in this box.
- Select 'Define Groups . . .', which opens the 'Two Independent Samples: Define Groups' sub-dialog box shown in Figure 18.3.
- Type '1' in the box beside 'Group 1:'.
- Select box beside 'Group 2:' and type '2'.

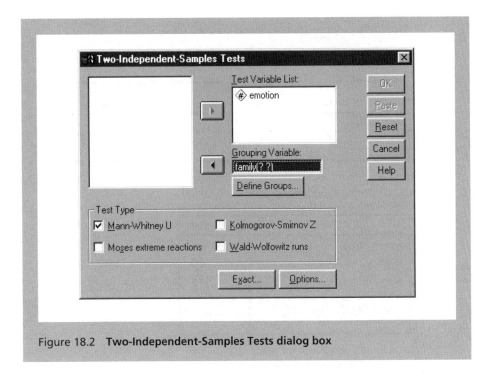

Figure 18.2   **Two-Independent-Samples Tests dialog box**

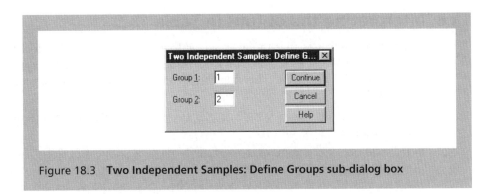

Figure 18.3   **Two Independent Samples: Define Groups sub-dialog box**

■ Select 'Continue', which closes the 'Two Independent Samples: Define Groups' sub-dialog box.

■ Select 'OK', which closes the Two-Independent-Samples Tests dialog box and the Data Editor window and which displays the output shown in Table 18.5.

Table 18.5 **Mann–Whitney U test output**

Ranks

	FAMILY	N	Mean Rank	Sum of Ranks
EMOTION 1		10	7.85	78.50
2		12	14.54	174.50
Total		22		

Test Statistics[b]

	EMOTION
Mann–Whitney U	23.500
Wilcoxon W	78.500
Z	−2.414
Asymp. Sig. (2-tailed)	.016
Exact Sig. [2*(1-tailed Sig.)]	.014[a]

a. Not corrected for ties.
b. Grouping Variable: FAMILY.

18.8 Interpreting the output in Table 18.5

■ The table indicates that the average rank given to 'EMOTION' for the first group (i.e. value = 1) is 7.85, and the average rank given to the second group (i.e. value = 2) is 14.54. This means that the scores for Group 2 tend to be larger than those for Group 1.

■ The basic Mann–Whitney statistic, the U value, is 23.500, which is statistically significant at the .014 level.

■ In addition, the computer has printed out a Z value of −2.414, which is significant at the .016 level. This is the value of the Mann–Whitney test when a correction for tied ranks has been applied. As can be seen, this has only altered the significance level marginally to .016 from .014.

18.9 Reporting the output in Table 18.5

We could report the results of this analysis as follows: "The Mann–Whitney U test found that the emotionality scores of children from two-parent families were significantly higher than those of children in lone-parent families ($U = 23.5$, $N_1 = 10$, $N_2 = 12$, two-tailed $p = 0.016$).".

Chapter 19

The variance ratio test: the *F*-ratio to compare two variances

■ *The variance ratio test (F-test) indicates whether two unrelated sets of scores differ in the variability of the scores around the mean (i.e. are the variances significantly different?).*

■ *This is clearly different from calculating whether two means are different and one should remember that variances can be significantly different even though the means for the two sets of scores are the same. Consequently, examining the variances of your variables can be as important as the comparison of the means.*

■ *The F-test is probably more commonly found associated with the t-test and the analysis of variance.*

19.1 Introduction

To compute the variance – or *F*-ratio – we divide the larger variance estimate by the smaller variance estimate. The variance estimate is produced by the 'Descriptives' procedure which we first introduced in Chapter 5. We will

Table 19.1 **Emotional stability scores from a study of ECT to different hemispheres of the brain**

Left hemisphere	Right hemisphere
20	36
14	28
18	4
22	18
13	2
15	22
9	1
Mean = 15.9	Mean = 15.9

illustrate the computation of the variance ratio with the data in Table 19.1 (*ISP* Table 19.2), which reports the emotional stability scores of patients who have had an electric current passed through either the left or the right hemisphere of the brain. In this chapter, the method involves a little hand-calculation. However, it provides extra experience with SPSS.

An alternative way of achieving the same end is to follow the *t*-test procedures in Chapter 13. You may recall that the Levene *F*-ratio test is part of the output for that *t*-test. Although Levene's test is slightly different, it is a useful alternative to the conventional *F*-ratio test.

19.2 Variance estimate

Quick summary

Enter data

Analyze

Compare Means

Means

Select variables ▶

Options

Variance

Continue

OK

■ Enter the data in Table 19.1 in the Data Editor as shown in Figure 19.1, putting the grouping variable ('spheres') in the first column (with '1' for 'left' and '2' for 'right') and the emotionality scores ('emotion') in the second column (as described in Chapter 13).

■ Select 'Analyze', which produces a drop-down menu (Figure 1.9).

■ Select 'Compare Means', which displays a second drop-down menu.

■ Select 'Means . . .', which opens the Means dialog box (Figure 19.2).

■ Select 'emotion' and the ▶ button beside 'Dependent List:', which puts 'emotion' in this box.

■ Select 'spheres' and the ▶ button beside 'Independent List:', which puts 'spheres' in this box.

■ Select 'Options . . .', which opens the 'Means: Options' sub-dialog box (Figure 19.3)

	spheres	emotion
1	1	20
2	1	14
3	1	18
4	1	22
5	1	13
6	1	15
7	1	9
8	2	36
9	2	28
10	2	4
11	2	18
12	2	2
13	2	22
14	2	1

Figure 19.1 **Emotional scores for two groups in the Data Editor**

- Select 'Variance' under 'Statistics:' and the ▶ button, which puts 'Variance' under 'Cell Statistics:'.
- Select 'Continue', which closes the 'Means: Options' sub-dialog box.
- Select 'OK', which closes the 'Means' dialog box and the Data Editor window and which displays the output shown in Table 19.2 in the Viewer window.

Table 19.2 **Estimated variance and the default descriptive statistics produced by the Means procedure**

Case Processing Summary

	Cases					
	Included		Excluded		Total	
	N	Percent	N	Percent	N	Percent
EMOTION * SPHERES	14	100.0%	0	.0%	14	100.0%

Report

EMOTION

SPHERES	Mean	N	Std. Deviation	Variance
Left	15.86	7	4.45	19.810
Right	15.86	7	13.84	191.476
Total	15.86	14	9.88	97.516

19.3 Calculating the variance ratio from output in Table 19.2

- Divide the larger variance estimate of Table 19.2 by the smaller variance estimate. The larger variance estimate is 191.476 (for 'Right'), which divided by the smaller one of 19.810 (for 'Left') gives a variance or F-ratio of 9.6656. This ratio is 9.66 when rounded *down* to two decimal places.

- We need to look up the statistical significance of this ratio in a table of critical values of F-ratios where the degrees of freedom for the numerator (191.48) and the denominator (19.81) of the ratio are both 6.

- The 0.05 critical value of the F-ratio with 6 degrees of freedom in the numerator and denominator is 4.28.

- The F-ratio we obtained is 9.66, which is larger than the 0.05 critical value of 4.28 (see *ISP* Significance Table 19.1 where the nearest critical value is 4.4 with 5 degrees of freedom in the numerator).

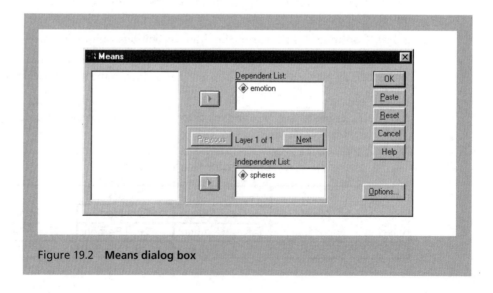

Figure 19.2   **Means dialog box**

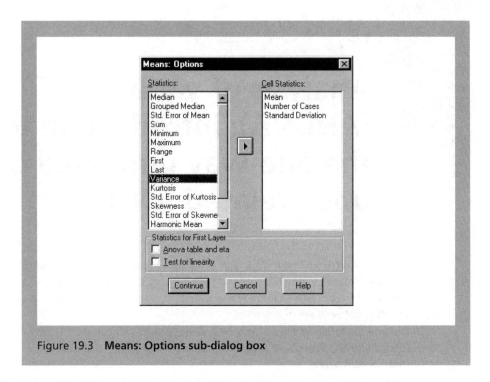

Figure 19.3   **Means: Options sub-dialog box**

19.4 Reporting the variance ratio

■ We would report these findings as: "The variance of emotionality scores of patients in the right hemisphere condition was significantly larger than those of patients in the left hemisphere condition ($F_{6,6} = 9.66$, $p < .05$).".

Chapter 20

Analysis of variance (ANOVA): introduction to the one-way unrelated or uncorrelated ANOVA

■ *The unrelated/uncorrelated analysis of variance tells you whether several (two or more) sets of scores have very different means. It assumes that the sets of scores come from different individuals. It is not essential to have equal numbers of scores for each set of scores.*

■ *The interpretation of the analysis of variance can be difficult with three or more sets of scores. It can be difficult to assess exactly where the differences lie in these circumstances.*

■ *For this reason, you may need to break the analysis down into several separate comparisons to assess which sets of scores are significantly different from which other sets of scores.*

■ *Ideally an adjustment should be made for the number of comparisons being made (see Chapter 23 on multiple comparisons for information on better methods for doing this than described in this chapter).*

We will illustrate the computation of a one-way unrelated analysis of variance with the data in Table 20.1 (*ISP* Table 20.2), which shows the scores of different participants in three conditions. It is a study of the effect of different hormone and placebo treatments on depression. So drug is the independent variable and depression the dependent variable. We have chosen to use the label 'cond' (short for 'condition' when labelling our data in Figure 20.1.

Table 20.1 **Data for a study of the effects of hormones**

Group 1 Hormone 1	Group 2 Hormone 2	Group 3 Placebo control
9	4	3
12	2	6
8	5	3

20.1 One-way unrelated ANOVA

Quick summary

Enter data

Analyze

Compare Means

One-Way ANOVA . . .

Dependent variable (e.g. 'depress')

▶

Independent or factor variable (e.g. 'cond')

▶

Options . . .

Descriptive

Homogeneity of variance

Continue

OK

- Enter the data in Table 20.1 in the Data Editor, putting the code for the three conditions (e.g. 1 for Group 1, 2 for Group 2 and 3 for Group 3) in the first column (called 'cond') and the score for each of the participants in those three conditions in the second column (called 'depress') as shown in Figure 20.1. Label the three conditions and remove the two zero decimal places.
- Select 'Analyze' on the menu bar near the top of the window, which produces a drop-down menu (Figure 1.9).
- Select 'Compare Means' from this drop-down menu, which opens a second drop-down menu.
- Select 'One-Way ANOVA . . .', which opens the One-Way ANOVA dialog box (Figure 20.2).
- Select 'depress' and the ▶ button beside 'Dependent List:', which puts 'depress' in this box.
- Select 'cond' and the ▶ button beside 'Factor:', which puts 'cond' in this box.
- Select 'Options . . .', which opens the 'One-Way ANOVA: Options' sub-dialog box shown in Figure 20.3.

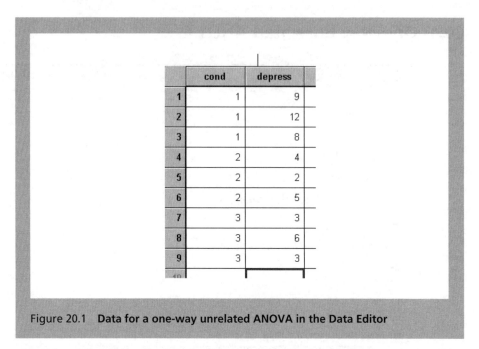

Figure 20.1   **Data for a one-way unrelated ANOVA in the Data Editor**

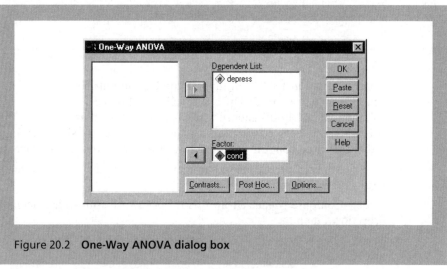

Figure 20.2   **One-Way ANOVA dialog box**

- Select 'Descriptive' and 'Homogeneity of variance'.
- Select 'Continue', which closes the 'One-Way ANOVA: Options' sub-dialog box.
- Select 'OK', which closes the One-Way ANOVA dialog box and the Data Editor window and which displays the output shown in Table 20.2.

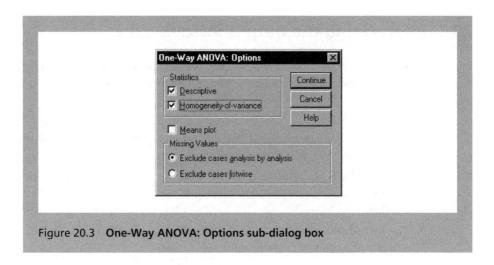

Figure 20.3   **One-Way ANOVA: Options sub-dialog box**

Table 20.2   **One-way ANOVA output**

Descriptives

DEPRESS

	N	Mean	Std. Deviation	Std. Error	95% Confidence Interval for Mean Lower Bound	95% Confidence Interval for Mean Upper Bound	Minimum	Maximum
Hormone 1	3	9.67	2.08	1.20	4.50	14.84	8	12
Hormone 2	3	3.67	1.53	.88	−.13	7.46	2	5
Placebo control	3	4.00	1.73	1.00	−.30	8.30	3	6
Total	9	5.78	3.31	1.10	3.23	8.32	2	12

Test of Homogeneity of Variances

DEPRESS

Levene Statistic	df1	df2	Sig.
.293	2	6	.756

ANOVA

DEPRESS

	Sum of Squares	df	Mean Square	F	Sig.
Between Groups	68.222	2	34.111	10.586	.011
Within Groups	19.333	6	3.222		
Total	87.556	8			

20.2 Interpreting the output in Table 20.2

■ The descriptive statistics are presented in the first table, the homogeneity test of variances in the second table and the analysis of variance table in the third table.

■ As the probability of Levene's test is non-significant, the variances are homogeneous (do not differ). Thus we can interpret the F-ratio without having to transform the data.

■ **The F-ratio is the Between Groups Mean Square divided by the Within Group Mean Square, which gives an F-ratio of 10.586 (34.111/3.222 = 10.5869).**

■ **The probability of this F-ratio is .011. In other words, it is less than the 0.05 critical value and so is statistically significant.**

■ This indicates that there is a significant difference between the three groups. HOWEVER IT DOES NOT NECESSARILY IMPLY THAT ALL THE MEANS ARE SIGNIFICANTLY DIFFERENT FROM EACH OTHER. IN THIS CASE, ONE SUSPECTS THAT THE MEANS 3.67 AND 4.00 ARE NOT SIGNIFICANTLY DIFFERENT.

■ Which of the means differ from the others can be further determined by the use of multiple-comparison tests such as the unrelated t-test. To do this, follow the procedure for the unrelated t-test described in Chapter 13. You do not have to re-enter your data. However, do an unrelated t-test defining the groups as 1 and 2, then redefine the groups as 1 and 3, and finally you would redefine the groups as 2 and 3. For our example, group 1 is significantly different from groups 2 and 3, which do not differ significantly from each other. (See *ISP* Chapter 13 for more details.)

■ Because we are doing three comparisons, the exact significance level of each t-test should be multiplied by 3 to obtain the Bonferroni significance level.

20.3 Reporting the output in Table 20.2

We could report the results of the output as follows: "The effect of the drug treatment was significant overall ($F_{2,6} = 10.58$, $p = 0.011$). When a Bonferroni adjustment was made for the number of comparisons, the only significant difference was between the means of hormone treatment 1 and hormone treatment 2 ($t = 4.02$, $df = 4$, two-tailed $p < .05$). The mean of hormone treatment 1 (M = 9.67, SD = 2.08) was significantly greater than that for hormone treatment 2 (M = 3.67, SD = 1.53). There was no significant difference between the mean of the placebo control and the mean of either hormone treatment 1 or hormone treatment 2.".

Chapter 21

Analysis of variance for correlated scores or repeated measures

■ *The correlated/related analysis of variance tells you whether several (two or more) sets of scores have very different means. However, it assumes that a single sample of individuals has contributed scores to each of the different sets of scores and that the correlation coefficients between sets of scores are large.*

■ *If your data do not meet these requirements then turn back to Chapter 20 on the unrelated analysis of variance.*

We will illustrate the computation of a one-way correlated analysis of variance with the data in Table 21.1, which shows the scores of the same participants in three different conditions (*ISP* Table 21.10).

Table 21.1   **Pain relief scores from a drugs experiment**

	Aspirin	**'Product X'**	**Placebo**
Bob Robertson	7	8	6
Mavis Fletcher	5	10	3
Bob Polansky	6	6	4
Ann Harrison	9	9	2
Bert Entwistle	3	7	5

21.1 One-way correlated ANOVA

Quick summary

Enter data

Analyze

165

General Linear Model

Repeated Measures . . .

Number of levels of factor (e.g. 3)

Add

Define

First variable/level (e.g. 'aspirin')

▶ *button beside Within-Subjects Variables:*

Repeat as necessary

Options

Descriptive statistics

Continue

OK

■ Enter the data in Table 21.1 in the Data Editor, putting the score for the first condition in the first column ('aspirin'), the score for the second condition in the second column ('productx') and the score for the third condition in the third column ('placebo') as shown in Figure 21.1.

■ Select 'Analyze' on the menu bar near the top of the window, which produces a drop-down menu (Figure 1.9).

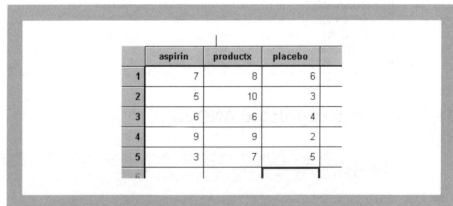

Figure 21.1   **Data for one-way correlated ANOVA in the Data Editor**

■ Select 'General Linear Model', which produces a second drop-down menu.
■ Select 'Repeated Measures . . .', which opens the Repeated Measures Define Factor(s) dialog box (Figure 21.2).
■ Type '3' in the box beside 'Number of Levels:' and select 'Add', which puts the expression 'factor1(3)' in the bottom box.

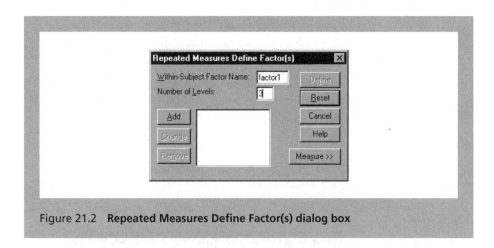

Figure 21.2   **Repeated Measures Define Factor(s) dialog box**

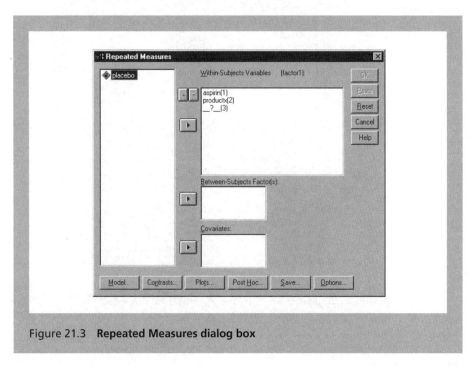

Figure 21.3   **Repeated Measures dialog box**

■ Select 'Define', which opens the Repeated Measures dialog box (Figure 21.3).

■ Select 'aspirin' and the ▶ button beside 'Within-Subjects Variables [factor1]:', which puts 'aspirin' in this box.

■ Repeat this procedure with 'productx' and 'placebo'.

■ Select 'Options', which opens the 'Repeated Measures: Options' sub-dialog box (Figure 21.4).

■ Select 'Descriptive statistics' in the Display section.

■ Select 'Continue', which closes the 'Repeated Measures: Options' sub-dialog box.

■ Select 'OK', which closes the Repeated Measures dialog box and the Data Editor window and which presents the output shown in Table 21.2 in the Viewer window.

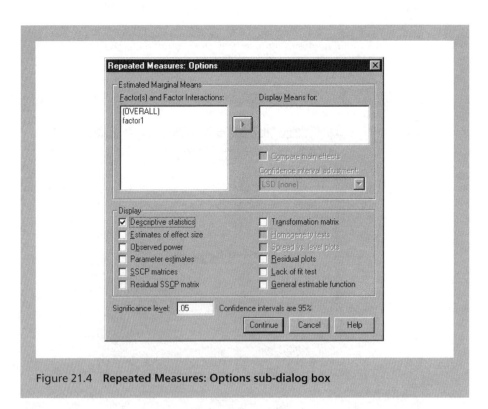

Figure 21.4   **Repeated Measures: Options sub-dialog box**

Table 21.2   **One-way correlated ANOVA output**

Within-Subjects Factors
Measure: MEASURE_1

FACTOR1	Dependent Variable
1	ASPIRIN
2	PRODUCT X
3	PLACEBO

Descriptive Statistics

	Mean	Std. Deviation	N
ASPIRIN	6.00	2.24	5
PRODUCT X	8.00	1.58	5
PLACEBO	4.00	1.58	5

Multivariate Tests[b]

Effect		Value	F	Hypothesis df	Error df	Sig.
FACTOR1	Pillai's Trace	.755	4.630[a]	2.000	3.000	.121
	Wilks' Lambda	.245	4.630[a]	2.000	3.000	.121
	Hotelling's Trace	3.087	4.630[a]	2.000	3.000	.121
	Roy's Largest Root	3.087	4.630[a]	2.000	3.000	.121

a. Exact statistic.

b.
    Design: Intercept.
    Within Subjects Design: FACTOR1.

Mauchly's Test of Sphericity[b]
Measure: MEASURE_1

Within Subjects Effect	Mauchly's W	Approx. Chi-Square	df	Sig.	Epsilon[a]		
					Greenhouse-Geisser	Huynh-Feldt	Lower-bound
FACTOR1	.862	.444	2	.801	.879	1.000	.500

Tests the null hypothesis that the error covariance matrix of the orthonormalized transformed dependent variables is proportional to an identity matrix.

a. May be used to adjust the degrees of freedom for the averaged tests of significance. Corrected tests are displayed in the layers (by default) of the Tests of Within Subjects Effects table.

b. Design: Intercept.
    Within Subjects Design: FACTOR1.

Tests of Within-Subjects Effects

Measure: MEASURE_1

Source		Type III Sum of Squares	df	Mean Square	F	Sig.
FACTOR1	Sphericity Assumed	40.000	2	20.000	5.106	.037
	Greenhouse-Geisser	40.000	1.758	22.752	5.106	.045
	Huynh-Feldt	40.000	2.000	20.000	5.106	.037
	Lower-bound	40.000	1.000	40.000	5.106	.087
Error(FACTOR1)	Sphericity Assumed	31.333	8	3.917		
	Greenhouse-Geisser	31.333	7.032	4.456		
	Huynh-Feldt	31.333	8.000	3.917		
	Lower-bound	31.333	4.000	7.833		

Tests of Within-Subjects Contrasts

Measure: MEASURE_1

Source	FACTOR1	Type III Sum of Squares	df	Mean Square	F	Sig.
FACTOR1	Linear	10.000	1	10.000	1.905	.240
	Quadratic	30.000	1	30.000	11.613	.027
Error(FACTOR1)	Linear	21.00	4	5.250		
	Quadratic	10.333	4	2.583		

Tests of Between-Subjects Effects

Measure: MEASURE_1
Transformed Variable: Average

Source	Type III Sum of Squares	df	Mean Square	F	Sig.
Intercept	540.000	1	540.000	249.231	.000
Error	8.667	4	2.167		

21.2 Interpreting the output in Table 21.2

■ As can be seen, SPSS produces a great deal of output for the Repeated Measures procedure.

■ The output which is of most interest to us is the fifth table entitled 'Tests of Within-Subjects Effects'.

■ Because Mauchly's Test of Sphericity (in the table above) is not significant ($p = .801$) we look at the lines of the fifth table labelled 'Sphericity Assumed'.

■ The F-ratio is the Mean Square (MS) for 'FACTOR1' (20.000) divided by Error(FACTOR1) Mean Square (3.917). It is 5.106 (20.000/3.917 = 5.1059).

- The exact significance level of this F-ratio is 0.037. Since this value is smaller than 0.05, we would conclude that there is a significant difference in the mean scores of the three conditions.

- In order to interpret the meaning of the ANOVA as it applies to your data, you need to consider the means of each of the three groups of scores which are displayed in the second table. They are 6.00, 8.00, and 4.00.

- You also need to remember that if you have three or more groups, you need to check where the significant differences lie between the pairs of groups. The related t-test procedure in Chapter 12 explains this. For the present example, only the difference between the means for 'Product X' and the 'Placebo' was significant. Because you are doing several t-tests, each exact probability for the t-tests should be multiplied by the number of t-tests being carried out. In our example, there are three comparisons, so each exact probability should be multiplied by 3. This is known as the Bonferroni adjustment or correction (*ISP* Chapter 23).

21.3 Reporting the output in Table 21.2

- We could describe the results of this analysis in the following way. "A one-way correlated analysis of variance showed a significant treatment effect for the three conditions ($F_{2,8} = 5.10$, $p = .037$). The Aspirin mean was 6.00, the Product X mean 8.00, and the Placebo mean was 4.00. None of the three treatments differed from one another with related t-tests when a Bonferroni adjustment was made for the number of comparisons.".

- This could be supplemented by an analysis of variance summary table such as Table 21.3. Drugs is FACTOR1 in the output, and Residual Error is Error(FACTOR1) from the fifth table in the output (Table 21.2).

Table 21.3 **Analysis of Variance summary table**

Source of variation	Sum of squares	Degrees of freedom	Mean square	F-ratio
Drugs	40.00	2	20.00	5.10*
Residual error	31.33	8	3.92	–

* Significant at 5% level.

Chapter 22

Two-way analysis of variance for unrelated/uncorrelated scores

■ *Two-way analysis of variance allows you to compare the means on the dependent variable when you have TWO independent variables.*

■ *If you have more than one DEPENDENT variable then you simply repeat the analysis for each dependent variable separately. On the other hand, if the several dependent variables are measuring much the same thing then they could be combined together into a single overall measure using the summing procedures described in Chapter 17.*

■ *With SPSS, you do NOT need equal numbers of scores in each condition of the independent variable.*

We will illustrate the computation of a two-way unrelated analysis of variance with the data in Table 22.1. The table shows the scores of different participants in six conditions reflecting the two factors of sleep deprivation and alcohol (*ISP* Table 22.11).

Table 22.1   **Data for sleep deprivation experiment: number of mistakes on video test**

| | **Sleep deprivation** | | |
	4 hours	**12 hours**	**24 hours**
Alcohol	16	18	22
	12	16	24
	17	25	32
No alcohol	11	13	12
	9	8	14
	12	11	12

22.1 Two-way unrelated ANOVA

Quick summary

Enter data

Analyze

General Linear Model

Univariate . . .

Dependent variable and ▶ button beside Dependent Variable:

Independent variable and ▶ button beside Fixed Factor[s]:

Continue

Repeat as necessary

Options . . .

Display Means for: (select factors and their interactions)

Continue

Descriptive statistics

Homogeneity tests

Continue

Plots . . .

Horizontal axis variable and ▶ button beside Horizontal Axis: (e.g. sleepdep)

Line variable and ▶ button beside Separate Lines: (e.g. alcohol)

Add

Continue

OK

■ Enter the data in Table 22.1 in the Data Editor as shown in Figure 22.1, putting the code for the three sleep deprivation conditions (e.g. 1 for 4 hours, 2 for 12 hours and 3 for 24 hours) in the first column ('sleepdep'), the code for the two alcohol conditions (e.g. 1 for alcohol and 2 for no alcohol) in the second column ('alcohol') and the score for each participant in those six conditions in the third column ('errors'). Label the values of the two conditions and remove the two decimal places for all three variables.

■ Select 'Analyze' on the menu bar near the top of the window, which produces a drop-down menu (Figure 1.9).

	sleepdep	alcohol	errors
1	1	1	16
2	1	1	12
3	1	1	17
4	2	1	18
5	2	1	16
6	2	1	25
7	3	1	22
8	3	1	24
9	3	1	32
10	1	2	11
11	1	2	9
12	1	2	12
13	2	2	13
14	2	2	8

Figure 22.1   **Data for a two-way unrelated ANOVA in the Data Editor for 14 of the 18 cases**

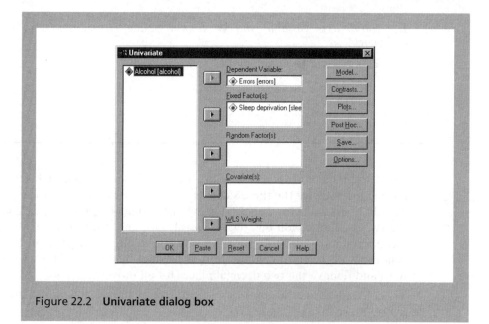

Figure 22.2   **Univariate dialog box**

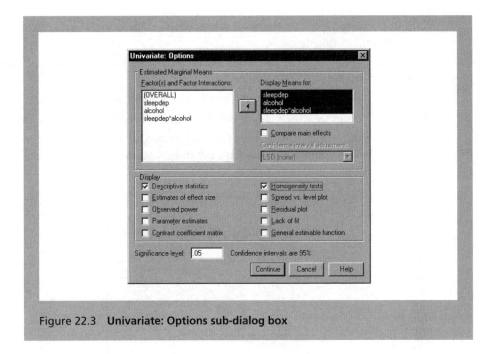

Figure 22.3   **Univariate: Options sub-dialog box**

- Select 'General Linear Model' from this drop-down menu, which opens a second drop-down menu.
- Select 'Univariate . . .', which opens the Univariate dialog box (Figure 22.2).
- Select 'errors' and the ▶ button beside 'Dependent Variable:', which puts 'errors' in this box.
- Select 'sleepdep' and the ▶ button beside 'Fixed Factor[s]:', which puts 'sleepdep' in this box.
- Select 'alcohol' and the ▶ button beside 'Fixed Factor[s]', which puts 'alcohol' in this box.
- Select 'Options . . .', which opens the 'Univariate: Options' sub-dialog box (Figure 22.3).
- Select 'sleepdep' in the text box under 'Factor(s) and Factor Interactions:' and the ▶ button beside it, which puts 'sleepdep' in the text box under 'Display Means for:' (Figure 22.3).
- Repeat this procedure for 'alcohol' and 'sleepdep*alcohol' (Figure 22.3).
- Select 'Descriptive statistics' and 'Homogeneity tests' in the Display section.
- Select 'Continue', which closes the 'Univariate: Options' sub-dialog box.
- Select 'Plots . . .' which opens the 'Univariate: Profile Plots' sub-dialog box shown in Figure 22.4.

- Select 'sleepdep' and the ▶ button beside 'Horizontal Axis:' which puts 'sleepdep' in this box.
- Select 'alcohol' and the ▶ button beside 'Separate Lines' which puts 'alcohol' in this box.
- Select 'Add' which puts 'sleepdep*alcohol' in the box under 'Plots:'.
- Select 'Continue' which closes the 'Univariate: Profile Plots' sub-dialog box.
- Select 'OK', which closes the 'General Factorial' dialog box and the Data Editor window and which displays the output shown in Table 22.2.

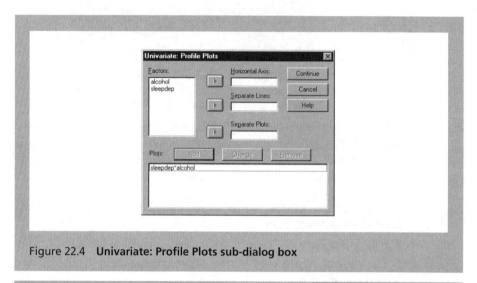

Figure 22.4   **Univariate: Profile Plots sub-dialog box**

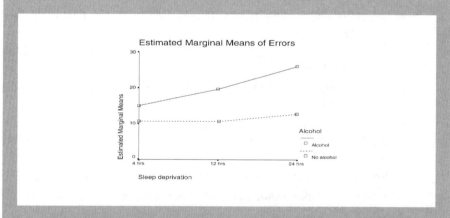

Figure 22.5   **Profile plot of errors for alcohol consumption and sleep deprivation**

Table 22.2   Two-way unrelated ANOVA output

Between-Subjects Factors

		Value Label	N
SLEEPDEP	1	4 hours	6
	2	12 hours	6
	3	24 hours	6
ALCOHOL	1	Alcohol	9
	2	No alcohol	9

Descriptive Statistics
Dependent Variable: ERRORS

SLEEPDEP	ALCOHOL	Mean	Std. Deviation	N
4 hours	Alcohol	15.00	2.65	3
	No alcohol	10.67	1.53	3
	Total	12.83	3.06	6
12 hours	Alcohol	19.67	4.73	3
	No alcohol	10.67	2.52	3
	Total	15.17	5.98	6
24 hours	Alcohol	26.00	5.29	3
	No alcohol	12.67	1.15	3
	Total	19.33	8.07	6
Total	Alcohol	20.22	6.10	9
	No alcohol	11.33	1.87	9
	Total	15.78	6.33	18

Levene's Test of Equality of Error Variances[a]
Dependent Variable: Errors

F	df1	df2	Sig.
2.786	5	12	.068

Tests the null hypothesis that the error variance of the dependent variable is equal across groups.
[a] Design: Intercept+SLEEPDEP+ALCOHOL+SLEEPDEP * ALCOHOL

Tests of Between-Subjects Effects
Dependent Variable: ERRORS

Source	Type III Sum of Squares	df	Mean Square	F	Sig.
Corrected Model	546.444[a]	5	109.289	9.739	.001
Intercept	4480.889	1	4480.889	399.287	.000
SLEEPDEP	130.111	2	65.056	5.797	.017
ALCOHOL	355.556	1	355.556	31.683	.000
SLEEPDEP * ALCOHOL	60.778	2	30.389	2.708	.107
Error	134.667	12	11.222		
Total	5162.000	18			
Corrected Total	681.111	17			

a. R Squared = .802 (Adjusted R Squared = .720).

Estimated Marginal Means

1. SLEEPDEP

Dependent Variable: ERRORS

SLEEPDEP	Mean	Std. Error	95% Confidence Interval	
			Lower Bound	Upper Bound
4 hours	12.833	1.368	9.854	15.813
12 hours	15.167	1.368	12.187	18.146
24 hours	19.333	1.368	16.354	22.313

2. ALCOHOL

Dependent Variable: ERRORS

ALCOHOL	Mean	Std. Error	95% Confidence Interval	
			Lower Bound	Upper Bound
Alcohol	20.222	1.117	17.789	22.655
No alcohol	11.333	1.117	8.900	13.766

3. SLEEPDEP * ALCOHOL

Dependent Variable: ERRORS

SLEEPDEP	ALCOHOL	Mean	Std. Error	95% Confidence Interval	
				Lower Bound	Upper Bound
4 hours	Alcohol	15.000	1.934	10.786	19.214
	No alcohol	10.667	1.934	6.453	12.881
12 hours	Alcohol	19.667	1.934	15.453	23.881
	No alcohol	10.667	1.934	6.453	14.881
24 hours	Alcohol	26.000	1.934	21.786	30.214
	No alcohol	12.667	1.934	8.453	16.881

22.2 Interpreting the output in Table 22.2

■ The descriptive statistics are displayed in the second table of the output as well as in the fifth, sixth and seventh tables. The means are portrayed graphically in Figure 22.5. The analysis of variance table is presented in the fourth table of the output.

■ In the second table the means, standard deviations and number of cases (N) for the two alcohol conditions for the first sleep deprivation condition ('4 hours') are shown first, followed by the means, standard deviations and number of cases for the two alcohol conditions for the second sleep deprivation condition ('12 hours').

■ Because the probability of Levene's test is non-significant (third table), we can interpret the F-ratios without having to transform the data.

■ In the analysis of variance table the F-ratio for the two main effects ('SLEEP-DEP' and 'ALCOHOL') is presented first.

■ For the first variable of sleep deprivation it is 5.797, which has an exact significance level of .017. In other words, this F-ratio is statistically significant at the 0.05 level, which means that the means of the three sleep conditions are dissimilar.

■ Which of the means differ from the others can be further determined by the use of multiple-comparison tests such as the unrelated t-test.

■ For the second variable of alcohol the F-ratio is 31.683, which is significant at less than the 0.0005 level. Since there are only two conditions for this effect we can conclude that the mean score for one condition is significantly higher than that for the other condition.

■ The means for the two factors ('sleepdep' and 'alcohol') and their interaction 'sleepdep*alcohol') are shown in the last three tables of Table 22.2.

■ The F-ratio for the two-way interaction between the two variables (SLEEP-DEP * ALCOHOL) is 2.708. As the exact significance level of this ratio is .107 we would conclude that there was no significant interaction.

22.3 Reporting the output in Table 22.2

■ We could report the results of the output as follows: "A two-way unrelated ANOVA showed that significant effects were obtained for sleep deprivation ($F_{2,12} = 5.80$, $p = 0.017$) and alcohol ($F_{2,12} = 31.68$, $p < 0.001$) but not for their interaction ($F_{2,12} = 2.70$, $p = .107$).".

■ It is usual to give an analysis of variance summary table. A simple one, like that shown in Table 22.3, would leave out some of the information in the third table in Table 22.2, which is unnecessary.

■ Because the 'sleepdep' factor has more than two conditions, we need to use an appropriate multiple-comparison test to determine the means of which groups differ significantly (see Chapters 21 and 23).

■ We also need to report the means and standard deviations of the groups which differ significantly. This can easily be done with the 'Means' procedure (section 19.2).

Table 22.3   Analysis of variance summary table

Source of variation	Sums of squares	Degrees of freedom	Mean square	F-ratio	Probability
Sleep deprivation	130.11	2	65.06	5.80	$< .05$
Alcohol	355.56	1	355.56	31.68	$< .001$
Sleep deprivation with alcohol	60.78	2	30.39	2.71	Not significant
Error	134.67	12	11.22		

Chapter 23

Multiple comparisons in ANOVA

■ *This chapter tells you how to work out which particular pairs of means are significantly different from each other in the analysis of variance.*

■ *It is used when you have more than two means.*

■ *This extends the coverage of multiple t-tests from Chapters 20 and 21.*

Knowing precisely where significant differences lie between different conditions of your study is important. The overall trend in the ANOVA may only tell you part of the story. SPSS has a number of 'post hoc' procedures which are, of course, applied after the data are collected and not planned initially. They all do slightly different things. There is a thorough discussion of them in Howell (1997). We will illustrate the use of these multiple-comparison procedures (using the data in Table 23.1, which were previously discussed in Chapter 20).

Table 23.1   Data for a study of the effects of hormones

Group 1 Hormone 1	Group 2 Hormone 2	Group 3 Placebo control
9	4	3
12	2	6
8	5	3

23.1 Multiple-comparison tests

Quick summary

Enter data

Analyze

Compare Means

One-Way ANOVA . . .

Dependent variable (e.g. 'depress')

Independent or factor variable (e.g. 'cond')

Post Hoc . . .

Duncan

Tukey

Scheffe

Continue

OK

- Enter the data as described in Chapter 20 (Figure 20.1) or retrieve the data file as described in Chapter 1.
- Select 'Analyze' on the menu bar near the top of the window, which produces a drop-down menu (Figure 1.9).
- Select 'Compare Means' from this drop-down menu, which opens a second drop-down menu.
- Select 'One-Way ANOVA . . .', which opens the One-Way ANOVA dialog box (Figure 20.2).
- Select 'depress' and the ▶ button beside 'Dependent List:', which puts 'depress' in this box.
- Select 'cond' and the ▶ button beside 'Factor:', which puts 'cond' in this box.
- Select 'Post Hoc . . .', which opens the 'One-Way ANOVA: Post Hoc Multiple Comparisons' sub-dialog box (Figure 23.1).
- Select Duncan, Tukey and Scheffe.
- Select 'Continue', which closes the 'One-Way ANOVA: Post Hoc Multiple Comparisons' sub-dialog box.
- Select 'OK', which closes the One-Way ANOVA dialog box and the Data Editor window and which displays the output shown in Table 23.2.

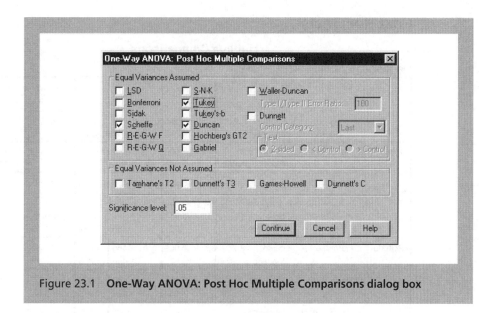

Figure 23.1 One-Way ANOVA: Post Hoc Multiple Comparisons dialog box

23.2 Interpreting the output in Table 23.2

■ The analysis of variance table is presented in the first table while the results for the three multiple-comparison tests are displayed in the second and third tables.

■ The *F*-ratio for the Between Groups effect (i.e. the effects of hormones) is 10.586, which has an exact significance level of .0108. In other words, the Between Groups effect is significant.

■ The last table, entitled 'Homogeneous Subsets', lists the sets of means which do not *differ* significantly from each other. So taking the section for Tukey HSD, there are two subsets of means. Subset 1 indicates that the Hormone 2 and Placebo control means of 3.67 and 4.00 do not differ significantly. Subset 2

Table 23.2 **Multiple-comparison tests**

ANOVA

DEPRESS

	Sum of Squares	df	Mean Square	F	Sig.
Between Groups	68.222	2	34.111	10.586	.011
Within Groups	19.333	6	3.222		
Total	87.556	8			

Post Hoc Tests

Multiple Comparisons

Dependent Variable: DEPRESS

	(I) COND	(J) COND	Mean Difference (I–J)	Std. Error	Sig.	95% Confidence Interval Lower Bound	95% Confidence Interval Upper Bound
Tukey HSD	Hormone 1	Hormone 2	6.00*	1.466	.015	1.50	10.50
		Placebo control	5.67*	1.466	.019	1.17	10.16
	Hormone 2	Hormone 1	−6.00*	1.466	.015	−10.50	−1.50
		Placebo control	−.33	1.466	.972	−4.83	4.16
	Placebo control	Hormone 1	−5.67*	1.466	.019	−10.16	−1.17
		Hormone 2	.33	1.466	.972	−4.16	4.83
Scheffe	Hormone 1	Hormone 2	6.00*	1.466	.018	1.30	10.70
		Placebo control	5.67*	1.466	.023	.97	10.37
	Hormone 2	Hormone 1	−6.00*	1.466	.018	−10.70	−1.30
		Placebo control	−.33	1.466	.975	−5.03	4.37
	Placebo control	Hormone 1	−5.67*	1.466	.023	−10.37	−.97
		Hormone 2	.33	1.466	.975	−4.37	5.03

*. The mean difference is significant at the .05 level.

Homogeneous Subsets

DEPRESS

	COND	N	Subset for alpha = .05 1	Subset for alpha = .05 2
Tukey HSD[a]	Hormone 2	3	3.67	
	Placebo control	3	4.00	
	Hormone 1	3		9.67
	Sig.		.972	1.000
Duncan[a]	Hormone 2	3	3.67	
	Placebo control	3	4.00	
	Hormone 1	3		9.67
	Sig.		.828	1.000
Scheffe[a]	Hormone 2	3	3.67	
	Placebo control	3	4.00	
	Hormone 1	3		9.67
	Sig.		.975	1.000

Means for groups in homogeneous subsets are displayed.
a. Uses Harmonic Mean Sample Size = 3.000.

contains just the Hormone 1 mean of 9.67. Thus the mean of Hormone 1 differs significantly from the means of both Hormone 2 and the Placebo control. However, the means of Hormone 2 and the Placebo control do not differ significantly. The pattern is identical for the Duncan and Scheffé tests in this case – it is not always so.

■ Therefore the three multiple-comparison tests all suggest the same thing: that there are significant differences between Hormone 1 and Hormone 2, and between Hormone 1 and the Placebo control. There are no other differences. So, for example, it is not possible to say that Hormone 1 and Hormone 2 are significantly different.

■ The choice between the three tests is not a simple matter. Howells (1997) makes some recommendations.

23.3 Reporting the output in Table 23.2

■ We could report the results of the output as follows: "A one-way unrelated analysis of variance showed an overall significant effect for the type of drug treatment (F_{226} = 10.59, p = 0.011). Scheffé's range test found that the Hormone 1 group differed from the Hormone 2 group (p = .018) and the Placebo Control (p = .023) but no other significant differences were found.".

23.4 Reference

Howell, D. (1997) *Statistical Methods for Psychology* (4th ed.). Boston: Duxbury Press.

Chapter 24

Analysis of covariance (ANCOVA) and two-way mixed analysis of variance (ANOVA) designs

■ *The analysis of covariance allows you to control or adjust for variables which correlate with your dependent variable before comparing the means on the dependent variable. These variables are known as covariates of the dependent variable.*

■ *To the extent that the levels of the covariates are different for your different research conditions, unless you adjust your dependent variable for the covariates you will confuse the effects of your independent variables with the influence of the pre-existing differences between the conditions caused by different levels of the covariates.*

■ *By controlling for the covariates, essentially you are taking their effect away from your scores on the dependent variable. Thus having adjusted for the covariates, the remaining variation between conditions cannot be due to the covariates.*

■ *A mixed analysis of variance design is merely a two-way (or three-way etc.) research design which contains BOTH unrelated and related independent variables.*

24.1 Introduction

One of the computations which are complex by hand but quick and easily done on SPSS is the analysis of covariance. This is much the same as the analysis of variance dealt with elsewhere but with one major difference. This is that the effects of additional variables (covariates) are taken away as part of the analysis. It is a bit like using partial correlation to get rid of the effects of a third variable on a correlation. We will illustrate the computation of an analysis of covariance (ANCOVA) with the data shown in Table 24.1, which are the same as those presented in Table 20.1 except that depression scores taken immediately prior to the three treatments have been included.

Table 24.1   **Data for a study of the effects of hormones (analysis of covariance)**

Group 1 Hormone 1		Group 2 Hormone 2		Group 3 Placebo control	
Pre	Post	Pre	Post	Pre	Post
5	9	3	4	2	3
4	12	2	2	3	6
6	8	1	5	2	3

It could be that differences in depression prior to the treatment affect the outcome of the analysis. Essentially by adjusting the scores on the dependent variable to 'get rid' of these pre-existing differences, it is possible to disregard the possibility that these pre-existing differences are affecting the analysis. So, if (a) the pre-treatment or test scores are correlated with the post-treatment or test scores, and (b) the pre-test scores differ between the three treatments, then these pre-test differences can be statistically controlled by covarying them out of the analysis.

24.2 One-way ANCOVA

Quick summary

Enter data

Analyze

General Linear Model

Univariate . . .

Dependent variable and ▶ button beside Dependent Variable:

Independent variable and ▶ button beside Fixed Factor[s]:

Covariate and ▶ button beside Covariate[s]:

Continue

Options . . .

Dependent variable

Continue

OK

■ Enter the data in Table 24.1 in the Data Editor as shown in Figure 24.1. The pre-test depression scores have been put into the third column ('pre_dep').

■ Select 'Analyze' on the menu bar near the top of the window, which produces a drop-down menu (Figure 1.9).

■ Select 'General Linear Model' from this drop-down menu, which opens a second drop-down menu.

■ Select 'Univariate . . .', which opens the Univariate dialog box (Figure 24.2).

■ Select 'post_dep' and the ▶ button beside 'Dependent Variable:', which puts 'post_dep' in this box.

■ Select 'cond' and the ▶ button beside 'Fixed Factor[s]:', which puts 'cond' in this box.

■ Select 'pre_dep' and the ▶ button beside 'Covariate[s]:', which puts 'pre_dep' in this box.

	cond	post_dep	pre_dep
1	1	9	5
2	1	12	4
3	1	8	6
4	2	4	3
5	2	2	2
6	2	5	1
7	3	3	2
8	3	6	3
9	3	3	2

Figure 24.1   **Post- and pre-depression scores in three treatments**

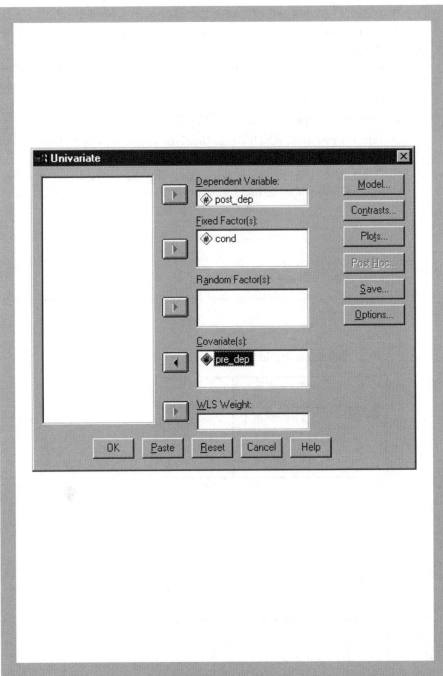

Figure 24.2   **Univariate dialog box**

■ Select 'Continue', which closes the 'Univariate: Model' sub-dialog box.

■ Select 'Options . . .' which opens the 'Univariate: Options' sub-dialog box (Figure 22.3).

■ Select 'cond' in the box under 'Factor(s) and Factor Interaction(s):' in the Estimated Marginal Means section (Figure 22.3) and the ▶ button, which puts 'cond' in the box under 'Display Means for:'.

■ Select 'Descriptive statistics' in the Display section.

■ Select 'Continue', which closes the 'Univariate ANOVA: Options' sub-dialog box.

■ Select 'OK', which closes the Univariate dialog box and the Data Editor window and which displays the output shown in Table 24.2.

Table 24.2   **One-way ANCOVA output**

Between-Subjects Factors

		Value Label	N
COND	1	Hormone 1	3
	2	Hormone 2	3
	3	Placebo control	3

Descriptive Statistics

Dependent Variable: POST_DEP

COND	Mean	Std. Deviation	N
Hormone 1	9.67	2.08	3
Hormone 2	3.67	1.53	3
Placebo control	4.00	1.73	3
Total	5.78	3.31	9

Tests of Between-Subjects Effects

Dependent Variable: POST_DEP

Source	Type III Sum of Squares	df	Mean Square	F	Sig.
Corrected Model	70.151a	3	23.384	6.718	.033
Intercept	27.684	1	27.684	7.953	.037
PRE_DEP	1.929	1	1.929	.554	.490
COND	26.425	2	13.213	3.796	.099
Error	17.405	5	3.481		
Total	388.000	9			
Corrected Total	87.556	8			

a. R Squared = .801 (Adjusted R Squared = .682).

Estimated Marginal Means

COND

Dependent Variable: POST_DEP

COND	Mean	Std. Error	95% Confidence Interval	
			Lower Bound	Upper Bound
Hormone 1	10.881a	1.955	5.856	15.906
Hormone 2	2.952a	1.443	−.756	6.661
Placebo control	3.500a	1.269	.237	6.763

a. Evaluated at covariates appeared in the model: PRE_DEP = 3.11.

24.3 Interpreting the output in Table 24.2

■ The unadjusted means are displayed in the second table of the output, the analysis of covariance table is presented in the third table of the output and the means adjusted for the covariate in the fourth table of Table 24.2.

■ The adjusted means of the three treatments are what the means are when all groups are adjusted to be identical on the covariate (in this case pre-treatment depression scores).

■ The adjusted mean is 10.881 for the first treatment, 2.952 for the second treatment and 3.500 for the third treatment.

■ We can see that these adjusted means seem to differ from the unadjusted means shown in the second table of the output. For the first treatment the adjusted mean is 10.88 and the unadjusted mean is 9.67. For the second treatment the adjusted mean is 2.95 and the unadjusted mean is 3.67, while for the third treatment the adjusted mean is 3.50 and the unadjusted mean is 4.00.

■ The F-ratio for the main effect is 3.796 ($13.213/3.481 = 3.796$).

■ The probability of this F-ratio is .099. In other words, it is greater than the 0.05 critical value and so is not statistically significant.

24.4 Reporting the output in Table 24.2

■ We could report the results of the output as follows: "A one-way ANCOVA showed that when pre-test depression was covaried out, the main effect of treatment on post-test depression was not significant ($F_{225} = 3.79$, $p = .099$). The covariate, pre-treatment depression-scores had a significant effect on post-treatment depression scores." You would normally also report the changes to the means once the covariate has been removed.

■ In addition, we would normally give an ANCOVA summary table as in Table 24.3.

Table 24.3   ANCOVA summary table for effects of treatments on depression controlling for pre-treatment depression

Source of variance	Sums of squares	Degrees of freedom	Mean square	F-ratio
Covariate (pre-treatment depression scores)	43.73	1	43.73	12.56*
Main effect (treatment)	26.43	2	13.21	3.80
Residual error	17.41	5	3.48	

* Significant at 5% level.

24.5 Two-way mixed ANOVA design

A two-way mixed analysis of variance has one unrelated factor and one related factor. Factors are independent variables. We will illustrate this analysis with the data in Table 24.4 (*ISP* Table 24.6), which consists of the self-esteem scores of children measured before and after an experimental manipulation in which half the children (chosen at random) were praised for good behaviour (experimental condition) while the other half were given no feedback (control condition).

Table 24.4   **Pre- and post-test self-esteem scores in two conditions**

Conditions	Children	Pre-test	Post-test
Control	1	6	5
	2	4	6
	3	5	7
Experimental	4	7	10
	5	5	11
	6	5	12

Quick summary

Enter data

Analyze

General Linear Model

Repeated Measures . . .

Number of levels of factor (e.g. 2)

Add

Define

First related variable (e.g. 'pretest')

▶ *button beside Within-Subjects Variables:*

Second related variable (e.g. 'posttest')

▶ *button beside Within-Subjects Variables:*

First unrelated variable (e.g. 'cond')

▶ *button beside Between-Subjects Factor(s):*

Repeat as necessary

Options

Descriptive statistics

Continue

Plots . . .

Horizontal axis variable and ▶ *button beside Horizontal Axis: (e.g. factor 1)*

Line variable and ▶ *button beside Separate Lines: (e.g. cond)*

Add

Continue

OK

	cond	pretest	posttest
1	1	6	5
2	1	4	6
3	1	5	7
4	2	7	10
5	2	5	11
6	2	5	12

Figure 24.3   **Data for a two-way mixed ANOVA in the Data Editor**

■ Enter the data in Table 24.4 in the Data Editor as shown in Figure 24.3, putting the values for the two conditions in the first column ('cond'), the pre-test scores in the second column ('pretest') and the post-test scores in the third column ('posttest'). Label the variables, the values of the two conditions and remove the two zero decimal places.

■ Select 'Analyze' on the menu bar near the top of the window, which produces a drop-down menu (Figure 1.9).

■ Select 'General Linear Model' from this drop-down menu, which opens a second drop-down menu.

■ Select 'Repeated Measures . . .', which opens the Repeated Measures Define Factor(s) dialog box (Figure 21.2).

■ Type '2' in the box beside 'Number of Levels:' and select 'Add', which puts the expression 'factor1(2)' in the bottom box.

■ Select 'Define', which opens the Repeated Measures dialog box (Figure 24.4).

■ Select 'pretest' and the ▶ button beside 'Within-Subjects Variables [factor1]:', which puts 'pretest' in this box. Do the same for 'posttest'.

■ Select 'cond' and the ▶ button beside 'Between-Subjects Factor(s):', which puts 'cond' in this box.

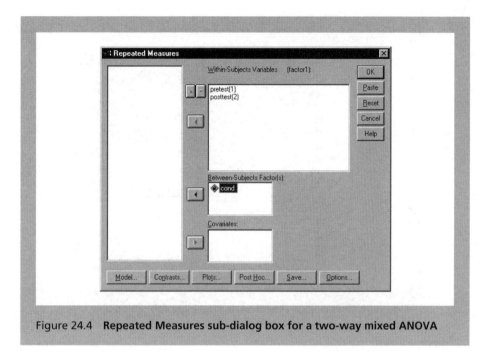

Figure 24.4   **Repeated Measures sub-dialog box for a two-way mixed ANOVA**

- Select 'Options . . .', which opens the 'Repeated Measures: Options' sub-dialog box (Figure 22.3).

- Select 'Descriptive statistics' in the Display section.

- Select 'Continue', which closes the 'Repeated Measures ANOVA: Options' sub-dialog box.

- Select 'Plots . . .' which opens the 'Repeated Measures: Profile Plots' sub-dialog box shown in Figure 24.5.

- Select 'factor1' and the ▶ button beside 'Horizontal Axis:' which puts 'factor1' in this box.

- Select 'cond' and the ▶ button beside 'Separate Lines' which puts 'cond' in this box.

- Select 'Add' which puts 'factor1*cond' in the box under 'Plots:'.

- Selct 'Continue' which closes the 'Repeated Measures: Profile Plots' sub-dialog box.

- Select 'OK', which closes the Repeated Measures dialog box and the Data Editor window and which presents the output shown in Table 24.5 in the Viewer window.

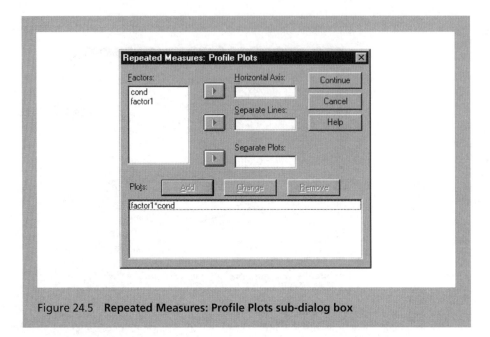

Figure 24.5   **Repeated Measures: Profile Plots sub-dialog box**

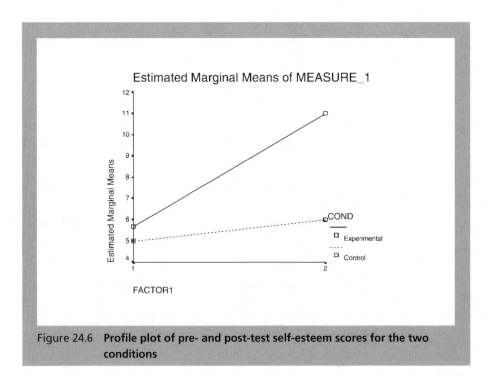

Figure 24.6   **Profile plot of pre- and post-test self-esteem scores for the two conditions**

Table 24.5   **Two-way mixed ANOVA output**

Within-Subjects Factors

Measure: MEASURE_1

FACTOR1	Dependent Variable
1	PRETEST
2	POSTTEST

Between-Subjects Factors

		Value Label	N
COND	1	Control	3
	2	Experiment al	3

Descriptive Statistics

	COND	Mean	Std. Deviation	N
PRETEST	Control	5.00	1.00	3
	Experimental	5.67	1.15	3
	Total	5.33	1.03	6
POSTTEST	Control	6.00	1.00	3
	Experimental	11.00	1.00	3
	Total	8.50	2.88	6

Multivariate Tests[b]

Effect		Value	F	Hypothesis df	Error df	Sig.
FACTOR1	Pillar's Trace	.804	16.409[a]	1.000	4.000	.015
	Wilks' Lambda	.196	16.409[a]	1.000	4.000	.015
	Hotelling's Trace	4.102	16.409[a]	1.000	4.000	.015
	Roy's Largest Root	4.102	16.409[a]	1.000	4.000	.015
FACTOR1 * COND	Pillar's Trace	.658	7.682[a]	1.000	4.000	.050
	Wilks' Lambda	.342	7.682[a]	1.000	4.000	.050
	Hotelling's Trace	1.920	7.682[a]	1.000	4.000	.050
	Roy's Largest Root	1.920	7.682[a]	1.000	4.000	.050

a. Exact statistic

b.

    Design: Intercept+COND

    Within Subjects Design: FACTOR1

Mauchly's Test of Sphericity[b]

Measure: MEASURE_1

Within Subjects Effect	Mauchly's W	Approx. Chi-Square	df	Sig.	Epsilon[a]		
					Greenhouse-Geisser	Huynh-Feldt	Lower-bound
FACTOR1	1.000	.000	0	.	1.000	1.000	1.000

Tests the null hypothesis that the error covariance matrix of the orthonormalized transformed dependent variables is proportional to an identity matrix.

a. May be used to adjust the degrees of freedom for the averaged tests of significance. Corrected tests are displayed in the layers (by default) of the Tests of Within Subjects Effects table.

b.
Design: Intercept+COND
Within Subjects Design: FACTOR1

Tests of Within-Subjects Effects

Measure: MEASURE_1

Source		Type III Sum of Squares	df	Mean Square	F	Sig.
FACTOR1	Sphericity Assumed	30.083	1	30.083	16.409	.015
	Greenhouse-Geisser	30.083	1.000	30.083	16.409	.015
	Huynh-Feldt	30.083	1.000	30.083	16.409	.015
	Lower-bound	30.083	1.000	30.083	16.409	.015
FACTOR1 * COND	Sphericity Assumed	14.083	1	14.083	7.682	.050
	Greenhouse-Geisser	14.083	1.000	14.083	7.682	.050
	Huynh-Feldt	14.083	1.000	14.083	7.682	.050
	Lower-bound	14.083	1.000	14.083	7.682	.050
Error(FACTOR1)	Sphericity Assumed	7.333	4	1.833		
	Greenhouse-Geisser	7.333	4.000	1.833		
	Huynh-Feldt	7.333	4.000	1.833		
	Lower-bound	7.333	4.000	1.833		

Tests of Within-Subjects Contrasts

Measure: MEASURE_1

Source	FACTOR1	Type III Sum of Squares	df	Mean Square	F	Sig.
FACTOR1	Linear	30.083	1	30.083	16.409	.015
FACTOR1 * COND	Linear	14.083	1	14.083	7.682	.050
Error(FACTOR1)	Linear	7.333	4	1.833		

Tests of Between-Subjects Effects

Measure: MEASURE_1
Transformed Variable: Average

Source	Type III Sum of Squares	df	Mean Square	F	Sig.
Intercept	574.083	1	574.083	1722.250	.000
COND	24.083	1	24.083	72.250	.001
Error	1.333	4	.333		

24.6 Interpreting the output in Table 24.5

■ As you can see, SPSS produces a considerable amount of output for this procedure.

■ The means, standard deviations and number of cases are shown in the second table of the output.

■ The F-ratio of particular interest to us is that for the interaction between the within-subjects and between-subjects factor which is displayed in the fifth and sixth table of the output. This F-ratio is 7.682 and has a probability value of .05. In other words, this interaction is just significant. If we look at the means for the four groups we can see that while the mean for the control condition increases little from pre-test (5.00) to post-test (6.00), the mean for the experimental condition shows a larger increase from pre-test (5.67) to post-test (11.00).

■ To determine whether these increases were statistically significant we could run a related t-test between the pre- and post-test scores for the two conditions separately (with Bonferroni adjustment for the number of comparisons carried out).

■ We could also see whether the two conditions differed at pre-test and at post-test with an unrelated t-test for the two test periods separately.

24.7 Reporting the output in Table 24.5

■ We could report the results of the output as follows: "The interaction between the two conditions and the change over time was statistically significant ($F_{1,4} =$ 7.68, $p = .05$). While the pre-test means did not differ significantly ($t = 0.76$, $df = 4$, two-tailed $p = .492$), the post-test mean for the experimental condition (M = 11.00, SD = 1.00) was significantly higher ($t = 6.12$, $df = 4$, two-tailed $p = .004$) than that for the control condition (M = 6.00, SD = 1.00). The increase from pre-test (M = 5.67, SD = 1.15) to post-test (M = 11.00, SD = 1.00) was significant for the experimental condition ($t = 4.44$, $df = 2$, two-tailed $p = .047$) but not for the control condition ($t = 1.00$, $df = 2$, two-tailed $p = .423$).".

Table 24.6   ANCOVA summary table for a two-way mixed design

Source of variance	Sums of squares	Degrees of freedom	Mean square	F-ratio
Between-subjects factor	24.08	1	24.08	72.25*
Between-subjects error	1.33	1	1.33	
Within-subjects factor	30.08	1	30.08	16.41*
Within-subjects error	7.33	4	1.83	
Interaction	14.08	1	14.08	7.68*

* Significant at .05 level.

■ An analysis of variance table for this analysis is presented in Table 24.6.
■ It is also useful to include a table of means (M) and standard deviations (SD) as shown in Table 24.7.

Table 24.7   Means and standard deviations of the pre- and post-tests for the control and experimental conditions

Conditions	Pre-test		Post-test	
	M	SD	M	SD
Control	5.00	1.00	6.00	1.00
Experimental	5.67	1.15	11.00	1.00

Chapter 25

Reading ASCII text files into the Data Editor

■ *Sometimes you have a computer file of data which you wish to use on SPSS. This chapter tells you how to use data not specifically entered into the SPSS Data Editor spreadsheet.*

25.1 Introduction

SPSS for Windows is obviously one of many different computer programs for analysing data. There are circumstances in which researchers might wish to take data sets which have been prepared for another computer and run those data through SPSS for Windows. It can be expensive in time and/or money to re-enter data, say, from a big survey into the Data Editor spreadsheet. Sometimes, the only form in which the data are available is as an archive electronic data file; the original questionnaires may have been thrown away. No matter the reason for using an imported data file, SPSS for Windows can accept files in other forms. In particular, data files are sometimes written as simple text or ASCII files, as these can be readily transferred from one type of computer to another. ASCII stands for American Standard Code for Information Interchange. To analyse an ASCII data file you first need to read it into the Data Editor.

Suppose, for example, that you had an ASCII data file called 'data.txt' which consisted of the following numbers:

1118
2119
3218

Obviously you cannot sensibly use an ASCII file until you know exactly where the information for each variable is. However, we do know where and what the information is for the small file above. The figures in the first column simply number the three different participants for whom we have data. The values in the second column contain the code for gender, with 1 representing females and 2 males. While the values in the third and fourth column indicate the age of the three people. We would carry out the following procedure to enter this ASCII data file into the Data Editor.

25.2 Reading an ASCII data file

Quick summary

File

Read Text Data

Disk drive, directory and file name of ASCII data file (e.g a:data)

Open

Next > (Repeat 3 times)

Click to indicate start of new variables

Next > (Repeat 2 times)

Finish

Yes

New file name

Save

■ Select 'File' from the menu bar near the top of the window to produce a drop-down menu (Figure 1.6).

■ Select 'Read Text File' which opens the Open File dialog box (Figure 25.1).

■ If you know the file name and its location, type in the disk drive, directory (if any) and file name of the ASCII data file (e.g. 'a:dat.txt') in the box beside 'File name:'. If you are uncertain of the file name and/or its location, select the 'Look in:' box which opens a drop-down menu with different locations on it. Note that if the name of your file does not end with the suffix '.txt', you need to select 'All files[*.*]' in the box beside 'Files of type:' to show files ending with this suffix. Once you have found the file name, select it.

■ Select 'Open' which closes the Open File dialog box and opens the Step 1 dialog box of the Text Import Wizard (Figure 25.2).

■ Select 'Next' to close this dialog box and to open the Step 2 dialog box. Repeat this twice to reach the Step 4 dialog box (Figure 25.3).

■ Click after the first column as this column contains the number of the participant. Click after the second column which holds the code for gender.

■ Select 'Next' to close the Step 4 dialog box and open the Step 5 dialog box. Repeat this to open the Step 6 dialog box.

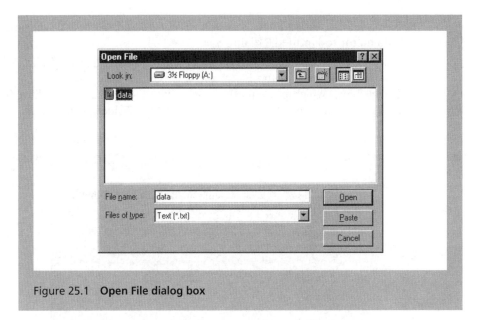

Figure 25.1   **Open File dialog box**

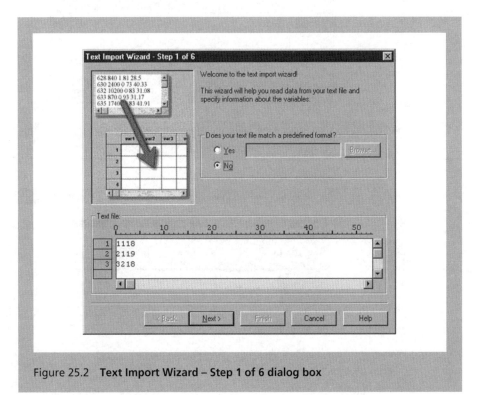

Figure 25.2   **Text Import Wizard – Step 1 of 6 dialog box**

■ Select 'Finish' to close the Text Import Wizard and to open 'Save contents of data editor to Untitled?' dialog box.

■ Select 'Yes' to open the Save Data As dialog box (Figure 1.7). Type in the location and name of the file in the box besides 'File name:' (e.g. 'a:data'). Select 'Save' which presents the ASCII data file in the Data Editor (Figure 25.4). You can now label the variables and their values (section 2.2).

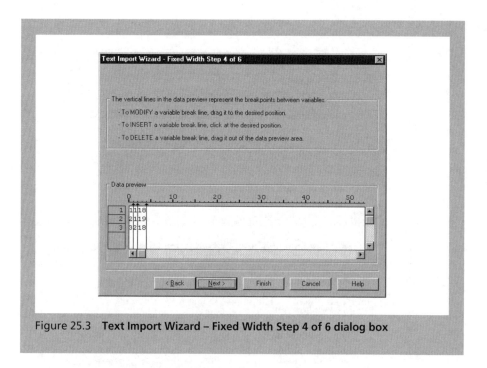

Figure 25.3   **Text Import Wizard – Fixed Width Step 4 of 6 dialog box**

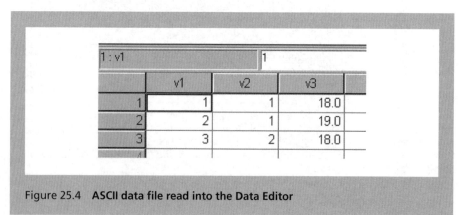

Figure 25.4   **ASCII data file read into the Data Editor**

Chapter 26

Partial correlation

■ *If you suspect that a correlation between two variables is affected by their correlations with yet another variable, it is possible to adjust for the effects of this additional variable by using the partial correlation procedure.*

■ *Using SPSS, it is also possible to simultaneously control for several variables which may be affecting the correlation coefficient.*

SPSS for Windows cannot easily compute partial correlations from a matrix of zero-order correlations. Consequently, we will illustrate the computation of partial correlations with the raw scores in Table 26.1, which represent a numerical intelligence test score, a verbal intelligence test score and age in years. We will correlate the two test scores partialling out age.

Table 26.1   Numerical and verbal intelligence test scores and age

Numerical scores	Verbal scores	Age
90	90	13
100	95	15
95	95	15
105	105	16
100	100	17

26.1 Partial correlation

Quick summary

Analyze

Correlate

Partial . . .

Variables and ▶ *Variables:*

Control variables and ▶ *Controlling for:*

OK

■ Enter the numerical intelligence test scores in the first column (called 'iq_numer') of the Data Editor, the verbal intelligence test scores in the second column (called 'iq_verb') and age in the third column (Figure 26.1). Label these three variables and remove the two zero decimal places.

■ Select 'Analyze' from the menu bar near the top of the window, which produces a drop-down menu (Figure 1.9).

■ Select 'Correlate' from the drop-down menu, which reveals a smaller drop-down menu.

■ Select 'Partial . . .' from this drop-down menu, which opens the Partial Correlations dialog box (Figure 26.2).

■ Select 'iq_numer' and 'iq_verb' and the ▶ button besides the 'Variables:' text box, which puts these two variables in it.

■ Select 'age' and the ▶ button besides the 'Controlling for:' text box, which puts 'age' in it. (You can include several other control variables at this point if they are available. For our example, however, we only have one.)

■ Select 'OK', which closes the Partial Correlations dialog box and the Data Editor window and which displays the output in Table 26.2 in the Viewer window.

	iq_numer	iq_verb	age	
1	90	90	13	
2	100	95	15	
3	95	95	15	
4	105	105	16	
5	100	100	17	

Figure 26.1   **Numerical and verbal intelligence scores and age in the Data Editor**

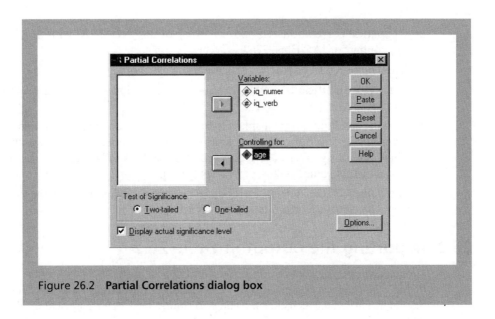

Figure 26.2   **Partial Correlations dialog box**

Table 26.2   **Partial correlation output**

---PARTIAL CORRELATION COEFFICIENTS---

Controlling for.. AGE

	IQ_NUMER	IQ_VERB
IQ_NUMER	1.0000	.7762
	(0)	(2)
	P= .	P= .224
IQ_VERB	.7762	1.0000
	(2)	(0)
	P= .224	P= .

(Coefficient / (D.F.) / 2-tailed Significance)
" . " is printed if a coefficient cannot be computed

26.2 Interpreting the output in Table 26.2

■ The variables on which the partial correlation was carried out are given both in the columns and in the rows. We have just two variables so a 2 × 2 correlation matrix is generated.

■ The print-out gives indications of how to read the entries in the table (Coefficient / (D.F.) / 2-tailed Significance)

■ The partial correlation (Coefficient) of 'IQ_NUMER' with 'IQ_VERB' controlling for 'AGE' is .7762.

■ The degrees of freedom (D.F.) are 2.

■ The exact significance level (2-tailed Significance) is given to three decimal places (P= .224).

■ Partial correlations are displayed in a matrix. The diagonal of this matrix (from top left to bottom right) consists of the variable correlated with itself, which obviously gives a perfect correlation of 1.0000. No significance level is given for this value, as it never varies (p= .).

■ The values of the partial correlations are symmetrical around the diagonal from top right to bottom left in the matrix.

26.3 Reporting the output in Table 26.2

If you calculate the correlation between numerical intelligence and verbal intelligence the Pearson correlation is 0.92. Bearing this in mind, we could report the results in Table 26.2 as follows. "The correlation between numerical intelligence and verbal intelligence is 0.92 (df = 3, two-tailed p = .025). However, the correlation between numerical intelligence and verbal intelligence controlling for age declines to 0.78, which is not significant (two-tailed p = .224). In other words, there is no significant relationship between numerical and verbal intelligence when age is controlled.".

Chapter 27

Factor analysis

- Factor analysis allows you to make sense of a complex set of variables by reducing them to a smaller number of factors (or supervariables) which account for many of the original variables. Although it is possible to obtain valuable insights from a matrix of correlations between several variables, the sheer size of the matrix may make this difficult even with a relatively small number of variables.

- Factor analysis is commonly used when trying to understand the pattern of responses of people completing closed-ended questionnaires. The items measuring similar things can be identified through factor analysis and, consequently, the structure of replies to the questionnaire.

- Factor analysis, however, includes a variety of techniques and approaches which you may find bewildering. We provide a 'standard' approach which will serve the purposes of most researchers well.

We will illustrate the computation of a principal components factor analysis with the data shown in Table 27.1, which consist of scores on six variables for nine individuals. This is only for illustrative purposes; it would be considered a ludicrously small number of cases to do a factor analysis on. Normally, you

Table 27.1 **Scores of nine individuals on six variables**

Individuals	Variable 1	Variable 2	Variable 3	Variable 4	Variable 5	Variable 6
1	10	15	8	26	15	8
2	6	16	5	25	12	9
3	2	11	1	22	7	6
4	5	16	3	28	11	9
5	7	15	4	24	12	7
6	8	13	4	23	14	6
7	6	17	3	29	10	9
8	2	18	1	28	8	8
9	5	14	2	25	10	6

should think of having at least two or three times as many cases as you have variables. The following is a standard factor analysis which is adequate for most situations. However, SPSS has many options for factor analysis.

27.1 Principal components analysis with orthogonal rotation

Quick summary

Enter data

Analyze

Data Reduction

Factor . . .

Variables ▶

Descriptives . . .

Coefficients

Continue

Extraction . . .

Scree plot

Continue

Rotation . . .

Varimax

Continue

Options . . .

Sorted by size

Continue

OK

■ Enter the data of Table 27.1 into the Data Editor as shown in Figure 27.1.

■ Select 'Analyze' from the menu bar near the top of the window, which produces a drop-down menu (Figure 1.9).

■ Select 'Data Reduction' from the drop-down menu, which reveals a smaller drop-down menu.

■ Select 'Factor . . .' from this drop-down menu, which opens the Factor Analysis dialog box (Figure 27.2).

	var00001	var00002	var00003	var00004	var00005	var00006
1	10	15	8	26	15	8
2	6	16	5	25	12	9
3	2	11	1	22	7	6
4	5	16	3	28	11	9
5	7	15	4	24	12	7
6	8	13	4	23	14	6
7	6	17	3	29	10	9
8	2	18	1	28	8	8
9	5	14	2	25	10	6
10						

Figure 27.1   **Six scores for nine individuals in the Data Editor**

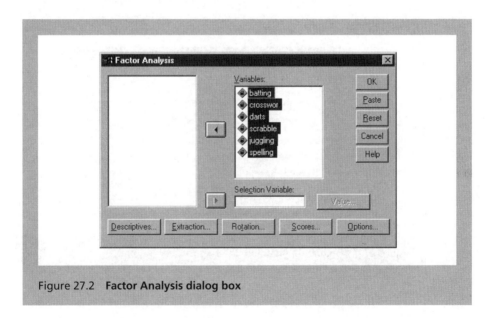

Figure 27.2   **Factor Analysis dialog box**

■ Select 'batting' to 'spelling' (pressing the left button on the mouse while holding down the Control key on the keyboard) and then the ▶ button, which puts these six variables in the 'Variables:' text box.

■ Select 'Descriptives . . .', which opens the 'Factor Analysis: Descriptives' sub-dialog box (Figure 27.3).

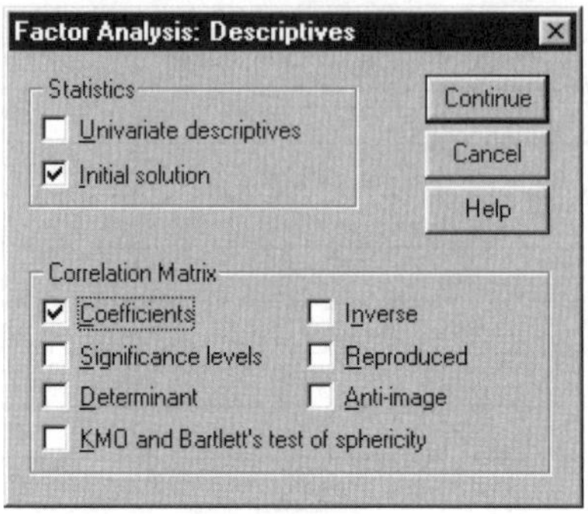

Figure 27.3   Factor Analysis: Descriptives sub-dialog box

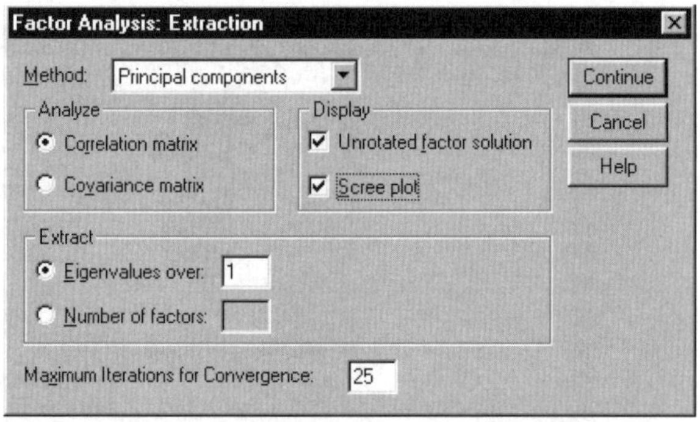

Figure 27.4   Factor Analysis: Extraction sub-dialog box

■ Select 'Coefficients' in the 'Correlation Matrix' section to obtain a correlation matrix of the six variables.

■ Select 'Continue' to close the 'Factor Analysis: Descriptives' sub-dialog box.

■ Select 'Extraction . . .', which opens the 'Factor Analysis: Extraction' sub-dialog box (Figure 27.4).

■ Select 'Scree plot'.

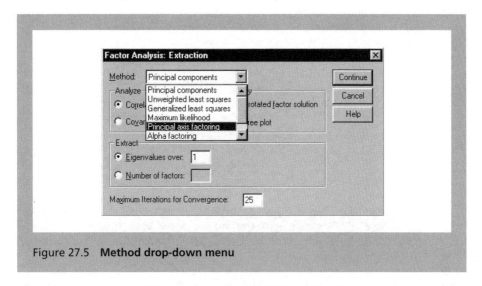

Figure 27.5   Method drop-down menu

Figure 27.6   Factor Analysis: Rotation sub-dialog box

■ As 'Principal components' is the default method we can proceed by selecting 'Continue' which closes the 'Factor Analysis: Extraction' sub-dialog box. If we wanted a different method, such as 'Principal axis factoring', we need to select 'Principal components' or the down-pointing arrow in the 'Method:' box which produces a drop-down menu to select from (Figure 27.5).

■ Select 'Rotation . . .' to open the 'Factor Analysis: Rotation' sub-dialog box (Figure 27.6).

■ Select 'Varimax' in the 'Method' section to obtain orthogonally rotated factors.

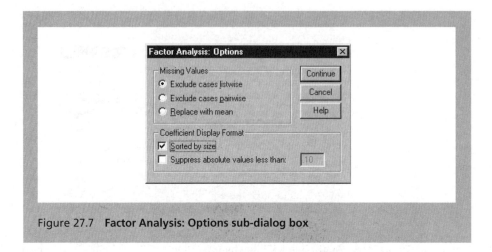

Figure 27.7   **Factor Analysis: Options sub-dialog box**

- Select 'Continue' to close the 'Factor Analysis: Rotation' sub-dialog box.
- Select 'Options . . .' to open the 'Factor Analysis: Options' sub-dialog box (Figure 27.7).
- Select 'Sorted by size' in the 'Coefficient Display Format' section to sort the factor loadings by size.
- Select 'Continue' to close the 'Factor Analysis: Options' sub-dialog box.
- Select 'OK', which closes the Factor Analysis dialog box and the Data Editor window and which displays the output in Table 27.2 in the Viewer window.

27.2 Interpreting the output in Table 27.2

- The first table presents the correlation matrix. From this it appears that there are two groups of variables that are strongly intercorrelated. One consists of batting, juggling and darts, and the other of crosswor, scrabble and spelling. Normally in factor analysis the correlation matrix is much more difficult to decipher than this. Our data are highly stylised.

- **The third table shows that two principal components factors were initially extracted in this case. The computer ignores factors with an eigenvalue of less than 1.00. This is because such factors consists of uninterpretable error variation. Of course, your analysis may have even more (or less) factors.**

- The Scree Plot also shows that a break in the size of eigenvalues for the factors occurs after the second factor: the curve is fairly flat after the second factor. Since it is important in factor analysis to ensure that you do not have too many factors, you may wish to do your factor analysis and rotation stipulating the number of factors once you have the results of the Scree test. [This

Table 27.2   **Principal components analysis output**

Correlation Matrix

		BATTING	CROSSWOR	DARTS	SCRABBLE	JUGGLING	SPELLING
Correlation	BATTING	1.000	.000	.910	−.047	.963	.096
	CROSSWOR	.000	1.000	.081	.883	.023	.795
	DARTS	.910	.081	1.000	−.005	.902	.291
	SCRABBLE	−.047	.883	−.005	1.000	−.080	.789
	JUGGLING	.963	.023	.902	−.080	1.000	.108
	SPELLING	.096	.795	.291	.789	.108	1.000

Communalities

	Initial	Extraction
BATTING	1.000	.961
CROSSWOR	1.000	.904
DARTS	1.000	.937
SCRABBLE	1.000	.910
JUGGLING	1.000	.959
SPELLING	1.000	.858

Extraction Method: Principal Component Analysis.

Total Variance Explained

Factor	Initial Eigenvalues			Extraction Sums of Squared Loadings			Rotation Sums of Squared Loadings		
	Total	% of Variance	Cumulative %	Total	% of Variance	Cumulative %	Total	% of Variance	Cumulative %
1	2.951	49.186	49.186	2.951	49.186	49.186	2.876	47.931	47.931
2	2.579	42.981	92.167	2.579	42.981	92.167	2.654	44.236	92.167
3	.264	4.401	96.567						
4	.124	2.062	98.630						
5	5.844E-02	.974	99.604						
6	2.378E-02	.396	100.000						

Extraction Method: Principal Component Analysis.

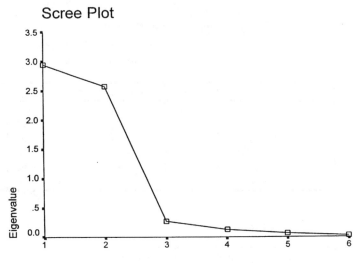

Scree Plot

Component Matrix[a]

	Component	
	1	2
DARTS	.907	−.340
BATTING	.870	−.451
JUGGLING	.870	−.451
SCRABBLE	.358	.884
CROSSWOR	.433	.847
SPELLING	.548	.747

Extraction Method: Principal Component Analysis.
   [a]. 2 components extracted.

Rotated Component Matrix[a]

	Component	
	1	2
BATTING	.980	−1.15E-02
JUGGLING	.979	−1.14E-02
DARTS	.962	.104
CROSSWOR	5.860E-03	.951
SCRABBLE	−7.76E-02	.933
SPELLING	.153	.914

Extraction Method: Principal Component Analysis.
Rotation Method: Varimax with Kaiser Normalization.
   [a]. Rotation converged in 3 iterations.

Component Transformation Matrix

Component	1	2
1	.893	.450
2	−.450	.893

Extraction Method: Principal Component Analysis.
Rotation Method: Varimax with Kaiser Normalization.

can be done by inserting the number in the 'Number of factors:' in the 'Factor Analysis: Extraction' sub-dialog box.] In the case of our data this does not need to be done since the computer has used the first two factors and ignored the others because of the minimum eigenvalue requirement of 1.00. It is not unusual for a component analysis to be recomputed in the light of the pattern which emerges.

■ **These two components are then orthogonally rotated and the loadings of the six variables on these two factors are shown in the fifth table entitled 'Rotated Component Matrix'.**

■ **The variables are ordered or sorted according to their loading on the first factor from those with the highest loadings to those with the lowest loadings. This helps interpretation of the factor since the high loading items are the ones which primarily help you decide what the factor is.**

■ On the first factor, 'batting' has the highest loading (.980) followed by 'juggling' (.979) and 'darts' (.962).

■ On the second factor, 'crosswor' has the highest loading (.951) followed by 'scrabble' (.951) and 'spelling' (.914). The apparent lack of difference in size of loading of 'crosswor' and 'scrabble' is due to rounding. This can be seen if you double click on the rotated component matrix table and then double click on these two loadings in turn.

■ We would interpret the meaning of these factors in terms of the content of the variables that loaded most highly on them.

■ The percentage of variance that each of the orthogonally rotated factors accounts for is given in the third table under '% of variance' in the 'Rotation Sums of Squared Loadings' section. It is 47.931 for the first factor and 44.236 for the second factor.

27.3 Reporting the output of Table 27.2

■ It would be usual to tabulate the factors and variables, space permitting. Since the data in our example are on various tests of skill, the factor analysis table might be as in Table 27.3. The figures have been given to two decimal places.

■ The exact way of reporting the results of a factor analysis will depend on the purpose of the analysis. One way of describing the results would be as follows. "A principal components factor analysis was conducted on the correlations of the six variables. Two factors were initially extracted with eigenvalues equal to or greater than 1.00. Orthogonal rotation of the factors yielded the factor structure given in Table 27.3. The first factor accounted for 48% of the variance and the second factor 44%. The first factor seems to be hand–eye coordination and the second factor seems to be verbal flexibility.". With factor analysis, since the factors have to be interpreted, differences in interpretation may occur.

Table 27.3   **Orthogonal factor loading matrix for six skills**

Variable	Factor 1	Factor 2
Skill at batting	0.98	−0.01
Skill at crosswords	0.01	0.95
Skill at darts	0.96	0.10
Skill at 'Scrabble'	−0.08	0.95
Skill at juggling	0.98	−0.01
Skill at spelling	0.15	0.91

Chapter 28

Stepwise multiple regression

■ *Stepwise multiple regression is a way of choosing predictors of a particular dependent variable on the basis of statistical criteria.*

■ *Essentially the statistical procedure decides which independent variable is the best predictor, the second best predictor, etc.*

28.1 Introduction

We will illustrate the computation of a stepwise multiple regression analysis with the data shown in Table 28.1, which consist of scores for six individuals on the four variables of educational achievement, intellectual ability, school motivation and parental interest respectively.

Table 28.1 **Data for stepwise multiple regression**

Educational achievement	Intellectual ability	School motivation	Parental interest
1	2	1	2
2	2	3	1
2	2	3	3
3	4	3	2
3	3	4	3
4	3	2	2

Because this is for illustrative purposes and to save space, we are going to enter these data 20 times to give us a respectable amount of data to work with. Obviously you would NOT do this if your data were real. It is important to use quite a lot of research participants or cases for multiple regression. Ten or 15 times your number of variables would be reasonably generous. Of course, you can use less for data exploration purposes.

28.2 Stepwise multiple regression analysis

Quick summary

Enter data

Analyze

Regression

Linear . . .

Criterion and ▶ beside Dependent:

Predictors and ▶ beside Independent[s]:

Enter in Method:

Statistics

R squared change

Continue

Stepwise

OK

■ Enter the data in Table 28.1 in the Data Editor, putting the scores for educational achievement in the first column (called 'achievem'), the scores for intellectual ability in the second column (called 'ability'), the scores for school

	achievem	ability	motivat	parental
1	1	2	1	2
2	2	2	3	1
3	2	2	3	3
4	3	4	3	2
5	3	3	4	3
6	4	3	2	2

Figure 28.1   Scores of four variables in the Data Editor

motivation in the third column (called 'motivat') and the scores for parental interest in the fourth column (called 'parental') as shown in Figure 28.1. Remove the two zero decimal places.

■ Carry out the instructions in the box *only if you are following the present particular analysis which enters the data 20 times. Otherwise ignore the box.*

■ In this particular analysis, because the size of the sample is too small for any of the predictors to explain a significant proportion of the variance in the criterion, we will increase the size of this sample 20 times by copying the data and pasting them in the first empty row 20 times using the 'Edit' option shown in Figure 28.2.

■ To do this, move the cursor to the cell in the first column of the first row in the Data Editor, press the left button of the mouse and, holding it down, move the cursor to the cell in the fourth column of the sixth row. The data are now highlighted.

■ Select 'Edit' to produce the drop-down menu shown in Figure 28.2.

■ Select 'Copy', which removes the drop-down menu.

■ Move the cursor to the cell in the first column of the seventh row.

■ Select 'Edit' to produce the drop-down menu again.

■ Select 'Paste', which removes the drop-down menu and inserts the copied material in the next six rows of the first four columns.

■ Repeat this procedure 20 times. Obviously you could reduce this repetition by copying each new set of data as it is produced, copying 12 rows the next time, 24 rows after that, and so on.

■ Alternatively it is most probably quicker to weight the six rows as described in Chapter 6.

■ Now return to the main instructions (select 'Analyze').

■ Select 'Analyze' from the menu bar near the top of the window, which produces a drop-down menu (Figure 1.9).

■ Select 'Regression' from the drop-down menu, which reveals a smaller drop-down menu.

■ Select 'Linear . . .' from this drop-down menu, which opens the Linear Regression dialog box (Figure 8.2).

■ Select 'achievem' and then the ▶ button beside the 'Dependent:' box, which puts 'achievem' in this box.

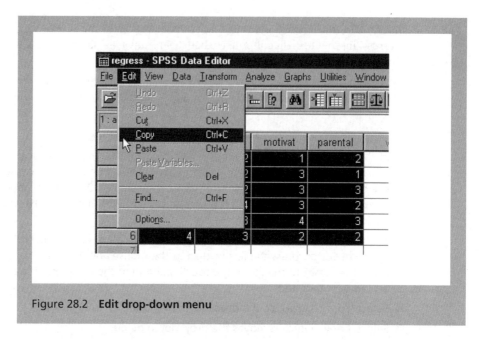

Figure 28.2   **Edit drop-down menu**

■ Select 'ability', 'motivat' and 'parental' and then the ▶ button beside the 'Independent[s]:' box, which puts these variables in this box.

■ Select 'Enter' or the down-pointing arrow in the 'Method:' box to produce a small drop-down menu.

■ Select 'Stepwise', which puts 'Stepwise' in the 'Method:' box.

■ Select 'Statistics', which opens the 'Linear Regression: Statistics' sub-dialog box (Figure 8.3).

■ Select 'R squared change'.

■ Select 'Continue', which closes the 'Linear Regression: Statistics' sub-dialog box.

■ Select 'OK', which closes the Linear Regression dialog box and the Data Editor window and which displays the output shown in Table 28.2 in the Viewer window.

28.3 Interpreting the output in Table 28.2

■ There is a great deal of information in Table 28.2. Multiple regression is a complex area and needs further study in order to understand all of its ramifications. In interpreting the results of this analysis we shall restrict ourselves to commenting on the following statistics: Multiple R, R Square, Adjusted R Square, Beta and R Square Change. Most of these are dealt with in a simple fashion in *ISP* Chapter 28. Points printed in bold are the most important.

Table 28.2   **Stepwise multiple regression analysis output**

Variables Entered/Removed[a]

Model	Variables Entered	Variables Removed	Method
1	ABILITY	.	Stepwise (Criteria: Probability-of-F-to-enter <= .050, Probability-of-F-to-remove >= .100).
2	MOTIVAT	.	Stepwise (Criteria: Probability-of-F-to-enter <= .050, Probability-of-F-to-remove >= .100).

a. Dependent Variable: ACHIEVEM.

Model Summary

Model	R	R Square	Adjusted R Square	Std. Error of the Estimate	R Square Change	F Change	df1	df2	Sig. F Change
					Change Statistics				
1	.701[a]	.491	.487	.69	.491	113.786	1	118	.000
2	.718[b]	.515	.507	.68	.024	5.850	1	117	.017

a. Predictors: (Constant), ABILITY.
b. Predictors: (Constant), ABILITY, MOTIVAT.

ANOVA[c]

Model		Sum of Squares	df	Mean Square	F	Sig.
1	Regression	54.000	1	54.000	113.786	.000[a]
	Residual	56.000	118	.475		
	Total	110.000	119			
2	Regression	56.667	2	28.333	62.156	.000[b]
	Residual	53.333	117	.456		
	Total	110.000	119			

a. Predictors: (Constant), ABILITY.
b. Predictors: (Constant), ABILITY, MOTIVAT.
c. Dependent Variable: ACHIEVEM.

Coefficients[a]

Model		Unstandardized Coefficients		Standardized Coefficients		
		B	Std. Error	Beta	t	Sig.
1	(Constant)	.100	.234		.428	.669
	ABILITY	.900	.084	.701	10.667	.000
2	(Constant)	−.167	.254		−.656	.513
	ABILITY	.833	.087	.649	9.561	.000
	MOTIVAT	.167	.069	.164	2.419	.017

a. Dependent Variable: ACHIEVEM.

Excluded Variables[c]

Model		Beta In	t	Sig.	Partial Correlation	Collinearity Statistics Tolerance
1	MOTIVAT	.164[a]	2.419	.017	.218	.900
	PARENTAL	.051[a]	.775	.440	.071	.988
2	PARENTAL	.000[b]	.000	1.000	.000	.882

a. Predictors in the Model: (Constant), ABILITY.
b. Predictors in the Model: (Constant), ABILITY, MOTIVAT.
c. Dependent Variable: ACHIEVEM.

■ Notice how badly the first table in particular is laid out. If you double click on a table it will be enclosed in a rectangle. To move any but the first line, move the cursor to that line. When it changes to a double-arrow (↔), click the left button of the mouse and, holding the left button down, move the line to the position you want before releasing the button. By dragging the column dividers in this way you should be able to obtain a better and more easily read table.

■ **The values of Multiple R, R Square and Adjusted R Square for the two steps (called Models) are summarised in the second table of the output entitled 'Model Summary'. Beta is presented in the fourth table of the output entitled 'Coefficients'.**

■ **The predictor that is entered on the first step of the stepwise analysis (Model 1) is the predictor which has the highest correlation with the criterion. In this example this predictor is 'ABILITY' (as indicated in note 'a' immediately underneath this table).**

- As there is only predictor in the regression equation on the first step, Multiple R is a single correlation coefficient. In this case it is .701 or 0.70 to two decimal places.

- **R Square is the multiple correlation coefficient squared, which in this instance is .491 or 0.49 to two decimal places. This indicates that 49% of the variance in the criterion is shared with or 'explained by' the first predictor.**

- **Adjusted R Square is R Square which has been adjusted for the size of the sample and the number of predictors in the equation. The effect of this adjustment is to reduce the size of R Square, so Adjusted R Square is .487 or 0.49 to two decimal places.**

- Beta in the table entitled 'Coefficients' is the standardised regression coefficient, which is the same as the correlation when there is only one predictor. It is as if all your scores had been transformed to z-scores before the analysis began.

- **The variable which is entered second in the regression equation is the predictor, which generally explains the second greatest significant proportion of the variance in the criterion. In this example, this variable is 'MOTIVAT'.**

- **The Multiple R, R Square and Adjusted R Square are .718, .515 and .507 respectively which, rounded to two decimal places, are 0.72, 0.52 and 0.51.**

- **In other words, the two variables of 'ABILITY' and 'MOTIVAT' explain or account for 51% of the variance in the criterion.**

- **R Square Change presented under 'Change Statistics' in the second table shows the increase in the proportion of the variance in the criterion variable ('ACHIEVEM') by predictors that have been entered after the first predictor ('ABILITY'). In this case there is only one other predictor ('MOTIVAT'). This predictor explains a further 2.4% of the variance in the criterion.**

- Beta is .649 for the first predictor ('ABILITY') and .164 for the second predictor ('MOTIVAT').

- The analysis stops at this point, as the third predictor ('PARENTAL') does not explain a further significant proportion of the criterion variance. Notice that in the final table of the output entitled 'Excluded Variables', 'PARENTAL' has a t value of .000 and a significance level of 1.0000. This tells us that 'PARENTAL' is a non-significant predictor of the criterion ('ACHIEVEM').

28.4 Reporting the output of Table 28.2

- There are various ways of reporting the results of a stepwise multiple regression analysis. In such a report we should include the following kind of statement. "In the stepwise multiple regression, intellectual ability was entered first and explained 49% of the variance in educational achievement ($F_{1,118} = 113.76$, $p < .001$). School motivation was entered second and explained a further 2% $(F_{1,117} = 5.85, p = .017)$. Greater educational attainment was associated with greater intellectual ability and school motivation.".

■ A table is sometimes presented. There is no standard way of doing this but Table 28.3 is probably as clear as most.

Table 28.3   **Stepwise multiple regression of predictors of educational achievement (only significant predictors are included)**

Variable	Multiple R	B	Standard error b	Beta	t	Significance of t
Intellectual ability	0.70	0.83	0.09	0.65	9.56	0.001
School motivation	0.72	0.17	0.07	0.16	2.42	0.05

Chapter 29

Hierarchical multiple regression

■ *Hierarchical multiple regression allows the researcher to decide which order to use for a list of predictors.*

■ *Rather than let the computer decide on statistical criteria, the researcher decides which should be the first predictor, the second predictor, and so forth.*

■ *This order is likely to be chosen on theoretical grounds.*

29.1 Introduction

We will illustrate the computation of a hierarchical multiple regression analysis with the data shown in Table 29.1, which consist of scores for six individuals on the four variables of educational achievement, intellectual ability, school motivation and parental interest.

Table 29.1　**Data for hierarchical multiple regression**

Educational achievement	Intellectual ability	School motivation	Parental interest	Social class
1	2	1	2	2
2	2	3	1	1
2	2	3	3	5
3	4	3	2	4
3	3	4	3	3
4	3	2	2	2

We have added a further variable, social class, which is on a scale of 1 to 5, with 5 being the highest social class. Hierarchical analysis is used when variables are entered in an order predetermined by the researcher on a 'theoretical' basis rather than in terms of statistical criteria. This is done by ordering the independent variables in terms of blocks of the independent variables, called Block 1, Block 2, etc. A block may consist of just one independent variable or several. In this particular analysis, we will make Block 1 social class ('CLASS'), which is essentially a demographic variable which we would like to control for. Block 2 is going to be intellectual ability ('ABILITY'). Block 3 is going to be school motivation ('MOTI-VATION') and parental interest ('PARENTAL'). The dependent variable or criterion to be explained is educational achievement ('ACHIEVEM').

In our example, the model essentially is that educational achievement is affected by intellectual ability, which is partly determined by motivational factors such as school motivation and parental interest. Social class is being controlled for in this model since we are not regarding it as a psychological factor.

When doing a path analysis, it is necessary to do several hierarchical multiple regressions. One re-does the hierarchical multiple regression using different blocks and in different orders so that various models of the interrelationships can be explored.

29.2 Hierarchical multiple regression analysis

Quick summary

Enter data

Analyze

Regression

Linear . . .

Criterion and ▶ beside Dependent:

Predictors and ▶ beside Independent[s]:

Statistics

R squared change

Continue

OK

■ Enter the data used in Chapter 28 in the Data Editor or retrieve the file if the data have been stored.

■ Add the data for social class, which is shown as a fifth variable in Figure 29.1. (The six rows have been weighted or re-entered 20 times to produce a sizeable number of cases. YOU WOULD NOT DO THIS NORMALLY. IT IS MERELY A WAY OF MAKING THE BURDEN EASIER and should only be used when reproducing our example.)

■ Select 'Analyze' from the menu bar near the top of the window, which produces a drop-down menu (Figure 1.9).

	achievem	ability	motivat	parental	class	freq
1	1	2	1	2	2	20
2	2	2	3	1	1	20
3	2	2	3	3	5	20
4	3	4	3	2	4	20
5	3	3	4	3	3	20
6	4	3	2	2	2	20

Figure 29.1   **Five variables and a weighting factor in the Data Editor**

■ Select 'Regression' from the drop-down menu, which reveals a smaller drop-down menu.

■ Select 'Linear . . .' from this drop-down menu, which opens the Linear Regression dialog box (Figure 8.2).

■ Select 'achievem' and then the ▶ button beside the 'Dependent:' box, which puts 'achievem' in this box.

■ Select 'class' and then the ▶ button beside the 'Independent[s]:' box, which puts 'class' in this box.

■ Select 'Next'. This makes Block 1, which consists only of 'class'. Keep an eye on the way in which the rectangle reading 'Block 1 of 1' changes over the next few steps. This will help you understand how the blocks are formed.

■ Select 'ability' and then the ▶ button beside the 'Independent[s]:' box, which puts 'ability' in this box.

■ Select 'Next'. This makes Block 2, which consists of only 'ability'.

■ Select 'motivat' and 'parental' and then the ▶ button beside the 'Independent[s]:' box, which puts these two variables in this box. We do not need to select 'Next' this time, but essentially we have made Block 3, which consists of the two variables, 'motivat' and 'parental'.

■ Select 'Enter' in the 'Method' box if not already pre-selected.

■ Select 'Statistics . . .', which opens the 'Linear Regression: Statistics' sub-dialog box (Figure 8.3).

■ Select 'R squared change'.

■ Select 'Continue', which closes the 'Linear Regression: Statistics' sub-dialog box.

■ Select 'OK', which closes the Linear Regression dialog box and the Data Editor window and which displays the output shown in Table 29.2 in the Viewer window.

Table 29.2 **Hierarchical multiple regression analysis output**

Variables Entered/Removed[b]

Model	Variables Entered	Variables Removed	Method
1	CLASS[a]	.	Enter
2	ABILITY[a]	.	Enter
3	MOTIVAT, PARENTAL[a]	.	Enter

a. All requested variables entered.
b. Dependent Variable: ACHIEVEM.

Model Summary

					Change Statistics				
Model	R	R Square	Adjusted R Square	Std. Error of the Estimate	R Square Change	F Change	df1	df2	Sig. F Change
1	.065[a]	.004	−.004	.96	.004	.497	1	118	.482
2	.714[b]	.509	.501	.68	.505	120.333	1	117	.000
3	.769[c]	.591	.577	.63	.082	11.500	2	115	.000

a. Predictors: (Constant), CLASS.
b. Predictors: (Constant), CLASS, ABILITY.
c. Predictors: (Constant), CLASS, ABILITY, MOTIVAT, PARENTAL.

ANOVA[d]

Model		Sum of Squares	df	Mean Square	F	Sig.
1	Regression	.462	1	.462	.497	.482[a]
	Residual	109.538	118	.928		
	Total	110.000	119			
2	Regression	56.000	2	28.000	60.667	.000[b]
	Residual	54.000	117	.462		
	Total	110.000	119			
3	Regression	65.000	4	16.250	41.528	.000[c]
	Residual	45.000	115	.391		
	Total	110.000	119			

a. Predictors: (Constant), CLASS.
b. Predictors: (Constant), CLASS, ABILITY.
c. Predictors: (Constant), CLASS, ABILITY, MOTIVAT, PARENTAL.
d. Dependent Variable: ACHIEVEM.

Coefficients^a

Model		Unstandardized Coefficients		Standardized Coefficients	t	Sig.
		B	Std. Error	Beta		
1	(Constant)	2.369	.205		11.543	.000
	CLASS	4.615E-02	.065	.065	.705	.482
2	(Constant)	.250	.241		1.036	.302
	CLASS	−.100	.048	−.140	2.082	.040
	ABILITY	.950	.087	.740	10.970	.000
3	(Constant)	−.562	.284		−1.984	.050
	CLASS	−.313	.068	−.439	−4.615	.000
	ABILITY	.938	.084	.730	11.180	.000
	MOTIVAT	.187	.068	.185	2.769	.007
	PARENTAL	.438	.130	.314	3.374	.001

a. Dependent Variable: ACHIEVEM.

Excluded Variables^c

Model		Beta In	t	Sig.	Partial Correlation	Collinearity Statistics Tolerance
1	ABILITY	.740^a	10.970	.000	.712	.923
	MOTIVAT	.395^a	4.319	.000	.371	.877
	PARENTAL	.179^a	1.291	.199	.119	.434
2	MOTIVAT	.224^b	3.265	.001	.290	.825
	PARENTAL	.359^b	3.808	.000	.333	.424

a. Predictors in the Model: (Constant), CLASS.
b. Predictors in the Model: (Constant), CLASS, ABILITY.
c. Dependent Variable: ACHIEVEM.

29.3 Interpreting the output in Table 29.2

■ As summarised in the second table of the output entitled 'Model Summary', the variable entered on the first block is 'CLASS' (social class). The Adjusted R Square for this block is effectively 0.0 (–.004), which means that social class explains 0% of the variance of educational achievement.

■ As shown in the third table of the output entitled ANOVA, the statistical significance of the F-ratio for this block or model is .482. As this value is above the critical value of 0.05, this means that the regression equation at this first stage does not explain a significant proportion of the variance in educational achievement. Notice that the Regression sum of squares + the Residual sum of squares add to 110. This total sum of squares is the same for all of the succeeding analyses of variance for later steps in the regression equation.

■ The variable entered on the second block is 'ABILITY' (intellectual ability). The Adjusted R Square for this block or model is .501, which means that intellectual ability together with social class explains 50.1% of the variance of educational achievement.

■ The statistical significance of the F-ratio for this block is .000. As this value is much lower than the critical value of 0.05, the first two steps of the regression equation explain a significant proportion of the variance in educational achievement. Notice that the sums of squares for the Regression and the Residual add to 110.

■ The variables entered on the third and final block are 'MOTIVAT' (school motivation) and 'PARENTAL' (parental interest). The Adjusted R Square for this block is .557, which means that all four variables explain 55.7% of the variance of educational achievement.

■ The F-ratio for this block is .000. As this value is much lower than the critical value of 0.05, the first three steps in the regression equation explain a significant proportion of the variance in educational achievement.

■ **The simplest interpretation of the output comes from examining the fourth table entitled 'Coefficients' of the output from Table 29.2. Especially useful are the Beta column and the Sig (of t) column. These tell us that the correlation (Beta) between 'CLASS' (social class) and 'ACHIEVEM' (educational achievement) is –.439, which is significant at the .000 level. Having controlled for social class, Block 1, the correlation between 'ABILITY' (intellectual ability) and 'ACHIEVEM' (educational achievement) is .730. This is also significant at the .000 level. Finally, having controlled for 'CLASS' (social class) and 'ABILITY' (intellectual ability), the correlations for each of the variables in Block 3 (school motivation and parental interest) with educational achievement ('ACHIEVEM') are given separately.**

29.4 Reporting the output of Table 29.2

■ There are various ways of reporting the results of a hierarchical multiple regression analysis. In such a report we would normally describe the percentage of variance explained by each set or block of predictors (from the value of the R Square).

■ One way of reporting these results is to state that: "In a hierarchical multiple regression, social class was entered first and did not explain a significant percentage of the variance in educational achievement ($F_{1,118} = 0.49$, $p = .482$). When intellectual ability was entered second, a significant increment of

51% of the variance ($F_{1,117}$ = 120.33, $p < .001$) was explained. When both school motivation and parental interest were entered third, a further significant increment of 8% of the variance ($F_{2,115}$ = 11.50, $p < .001$) was explained.".

■ One would also need to summarise the regression equation as in Table 29.3.

Table 29.3   **Hierarchical multiple regression of predictors of educational achievement**

Blocks	B	Standard error B	Beta
Block 1:			
Social class	−.31	.07	−.44*
Block 2:			
Intellectual ability	.94	.08	.73*
Block 3:			
School motivation	.19	.07	.19*
Parental interest	.44	.13	.31*

* Significant at .01.

Chapter 30

Item reliability and inter-rater agreement

■ Reliability is a complex matter, as the term refers to a range of very different concepts and measures.

■ Item alpha reliability and split-half reliability assess the internal consistency of the items in a questionnaire — that is, do the items tend to be measuring much the same thing?

■ Split-half reliability on SPSS refers to the correlation between scores based on the first half of items you list for inclusion and the second half of the items. This correlation is adjusted statistically to maintain the original questionnaire length.

■ Coefficient alpha is merely the average of all possible split-half reliabilities for the questionnaire and so may be preferred, as it is not dependent on how the items are ordered. Coefficient alpha can be used as a means of shortening a questionnaire while maintaining or improving its internal reliability.

■ Inter-rater reliability (here assessed by Kappa) is essentially a measure of agreement between the ratings of two different raters. Thus it is particularly useful for assessing codings or ratings by 'experts' of aspects of open-ended data; in other words, the quantification of qualitative data. It involves the extent of exact agreement between raters on their ratings compared to what agreement would be expected by chance. Note then that it is different from the correlation between raters, which does not require EXACT agreement to achieve high correlations but merely that the ratings increase relatively for both raters.

Table 30.1 Data for 10 cases from a four-item questionnaire

Cases	Item 1	Item 2	Item 3	Item 4
1	1	3	5	6
2	2	1	1	2
3	1	1	1	1
4	5	2	4	2
5	6	4	3	2
6	5	4	5	6
7	4	5	3	2
8	2	1	2	1
9	1	2	1	1
10	1	1	2	2

30.1 Item alpha reliability

The answers of 10 people to the four items of a questionnaire are shown in Table 30.1. These data will be used to illustrate two measures of item reliability known as alpha reliability and split-half reliability.

Quick summary

Enter data

Analyze

Scale

Reliability Analysis . . .

items

Statistics

Scale if item deleted

Continue

OK

- As described in Chapter 1, enter the data of Table 30.1 into the Data Editor, putting item 1 responses into the first column, item 2 responses into the second column, and so on as shown in Figure 30.1. Label the four columns and remove the two zero decimal places.
- Select 'Analyze' from the menu bar near the top of the window, which produces a drop-down menu (Figure 1.9).
- Select 'Scale', which opens a further drop-down menu with two options.
- Select 'Reliability Analysis . . .', which opens the Reliability Analysis dialog box (Figure 30.2).
- Select 'item1' to 'item4' and the ▶ button, which puts these variables in the box beneath 'Items:'.
- Select 'Statistics . . .', which opens the 'Reliability Analysis: Statistics' sub-dialog box (Figure 30.3).
- Select 'Scale if item deleted'.

	item1	item2	item3	item4
1	1	3	5	6
2	2	1	1	2
3	1	1	1	1
4	5	2	4	2
5	6	4	3	2
6	5	4	5	6
7	4	5	3	2
8	2	1	2	1
9	1	2	1	1
10	1	1	2	2

Figure 30.1   **Responses to a four-item questionnaire in the Data Editor**

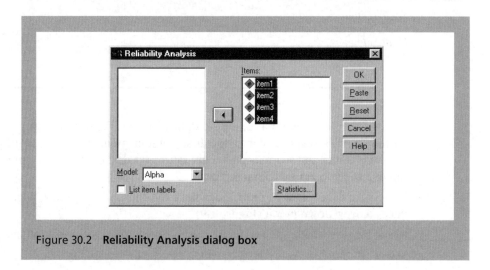

Figure 30.2   **Reliability Analysis dialog box**

■ Select 'Continue', which closes the 'Reliability Analysis: Statistics' sub-dialog box.

■ Select 'OK', which closes the Reliability Analysis dialog box and which displays the output shown in Table 30.2 in the Viewer window.

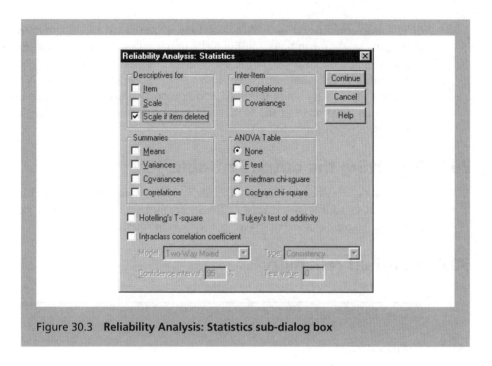

Figure 30.3   **Reliability Analysis: Statistics sub-dialog box**

Table 30.2   **Alpha reliability output**

R E L I A B I L I T Y   A N A L Y S I S   –   S C A L E   (A L P H A)

Item-total Statistics

	Scale Mean if Item Deleted	Scale Variance if Item Deleted	Corrected Item- Total Correlation	Alpha if Item Deleted
ITEM1	7.6000	18.9333	.4905	.8398
ITEM2	8.0000	19.5556	.7176	.7313
ITEM3	7.7000	17.7889	.8423	.6708
ITEM4	7.9000	18.7667	.5466	.8064

Reliability Coefficients

N of Cases = 10.0   N of Items = 4

Alpha = .8111

30.2 Interpreting the output in Table 30.2

■ The alpha reliability of the four items for the 10 cases is shown on the last line of the output in Table 30.2 and is .8111, which rounded to two decimal places is .81.

■ The last column entitled 'Alpha if Item Deleted' in the upper part of the output shows the alpha reliability if the item on that line is not included. From this column we can see that if we remove the first item ('item1'), the alpha reliability of the remaining three items of the scale increases slightly to .8398. Since this is a very small increase, it is not worthwhile dropping this first item from this short scale. If the scale was too long or unreliable, deleting items on this basis is appropriate.

30.3 Reporting the output in Table 30.2

One way of reporting the results of this analysis is as follows: "The alpha reliability of the four item scale was .81, indicating that the scale had good reliability.". An alpha of .70 or above is considered satisfactory.

30.4 Split-half reliability

Quick summary

Enter data

Analyze

Scale

Reliability Analysis . . .

items

Statistics

Alpha

Split-half

OK

■ The split-half reliability can be obtained by selecting 'Alpha' on the down-facing arrow in the box beside 'Model:' in the Reliability Analysis dialog box, which opens a small drop-down menu.

■ Select 'Split-half' from this menu.

■ Select 'OK', which closes the 'Reliability Analysis' dialog box and which displays the output shown in Table 30.3 in the Viewer window.

Table 30.3   **Split-half reliability output**

R E L I A B I L I T Y   A N A L Y S I S   –   S C A L E   (S P L I T)

Reliability Coefficients

N of Cases = 10.0		N of Items = 4	
Correlation between forms =	.4774	Equal-length Spearman-Brown =	.6463
Guttman Split-half =	.6459	Unequal-length Spearman-Brown =	.6463
2 Items in part 1		2 Items in part 2	
Alpha for part 1 =	.7773	Alpha for part 2 =	.9036

30.5 Interpreting the output in Table 30.3

The (Guttman) split reliability of the four items for the 10 cases is shown in the output in Table 30.3 as .6459, which rounded to two decimal places is .65.

30.6 Reporting the output in Table 30.3

One way of reporting the results of this analysis is as follows: "The split-half reliability of the four item scale was .65, indicating that the scale had only moderate reliability.".

30.7 Inter-rater agreement (Kappa)

Quick summary

Analyze

Descriptive Statistics

Crosstabs . . .

first rater (e.g. 'forensic')

▶ *Row[s]:*

second rater (e.g. 'psychiat')

▶ *Column[s]:*

Statistics . . .

Kappa

Continue

OK

Kappa is used to measure the agreement between two raters, taking into account the agreement that would be expected by chance. We will illustrate its computation for the data of Table 30.4, which shows the ratings by a forensic psychologist and a psychiatrist of 12 sex offenders in terms of the offenders being no risk (1), a moderate risk (2) or a high risk (3) to the public.

Table 30.4   **Ratings of risk by two professionals of 12 offenders**

Sex offenders	Forensic psychologist	Psychiatrist
1	3	3
2	3	3
3	3	3
4	1	1
5	1	2
6	3	3
7	2	3
8	3	3
9	2	3
10	3	3
11	3	3
12	3	3

■ Type the data in Table 30.4 into the Data Editor as shown in Figure 30.4 with the ratings for the forensic psychologist in the first column (called 'forensic') and those of the psychiatrist in the second column (called 'psychiat').

■ Select 'Statistics' from the menu bar near the top of the window, which produces a drop-down menu (Figure 1.9).

■ Select 'Summarize . . .', which opens another drop-down menu (Figure 1.9).

■ Select 'Crosstabs . . .', which opens the Crosstabs dialog box (Figure 14.3).

■ Select 'forensic' and then the ▶ button beside 'Row[s]:', which puts 'forensic' in this box.

■ Select 'psychiat' and then the ▶ button beside 'Column[s]:', which puts 'psychiat' in this box.

	forensic	psychiat
1	3	3
2	3	3
3	3	3
4	1	1
5	1	2
6	3	3
7	2	3
8	3	3
9	2	3
10	3	3
11	3	3
12	3	3

Figure 30.4 Rating data in the Data Editor

■ Select 'Statistics . . .', which opens the 'Crosstabs: Statistics' sub-dialog box (Figure 14.4).

■ Select 'Kappa'.

■ Select 'Continue', which closes the 'Crosstabs: Statistics' sub-dialog box.

■ Select 'OK', which closes the Crosstabs dialog box and which displays the output in Table 30.5 in the Viewer window.

30.8 Interpreting the output in Table 30.5

■ The data in Table 30.4 have been arranged into a 2 × 2 contingency in the second table of the output in Table 30.5. The number of cases on which the forensic psychologist and the psychiatrist agree are shown in the diagonal cells of this table. They are 1 for the rating of 1, 0 for the rating of 2, and 8 for the rating of 3.

■ Kappa is shown as .400 in the third table of the output. Although Kappa is statistically significant with $p = .046$, it indicates only moderate agreement.

■ Note that Kappa allows for raters tending to use the same ratings most of the time. It is NOT a measure of percentage agreement.

Table 30.5 **Kappa output**

Case Processing Summary

	Cases					
	Valid		Missing		Total	
	N	Percent	N	Percent	N	Percent
FORENSIC * PSYCHIAT	12	100.0%	0	.0%	12	100.0%

FORENSIC * PSYCHIAT Crosstabulation

Count

		PSYCHIAT			
		1	2	3	Total
FORENSIC	1	1	1		2
	2			2	2
	3			8	8
Total		1	1	10	12

Symmetric Measures

		Value	Asymp. Std. Error[a]	Approx. T[b]	Approx. Sig.
Measure of Agreement	Kappa	.400	.219	2.000	.046
N of Valid Cases		12			

a. Not assuming the null hypothesis.
b. Using the asymptotic standard error assuming the null hypothesis.

30.9 Reporting the output in Table 30.5

One way of reporting the results of this analysis is as follows: "Kappa for the agreement between the ratings of the forensic psychologist and the psychiatrist was .40, which indicates only moderate agreement.".

Chapter 31

Log-linear analysis

■ Log-linear analysis is used to analyse contingency tables consisting of three or more variables.

■ Its purpose is to determine which of the variables and their interactions best explain (or reproduce) the observed frequencies in the table. Variables and their interactions on their own and in combination are known as models.

■ Goodness-of-fit test statistics are used to assess the degree of correspondence between the model and the data. Statistical significance indicates that the model being examined fails to account totally for the observed frequencies. Statistical non-significance means that the model being analysed fits the observed frequencies. If more than one model fits the data well, the model having the fewer or fewest variables and interactions is the simplest one and may be the preferred model. Likelihood ratio Chi-square is employed as the test statistic.

We will illustrate the computation of a log-linear analysis with the data in Table 31.1. This table shows the frequency of sexual and physical abuse in 140 female and 160 male psychiatric patients. To analyse a table of data like this one with SPSS we first have to input the data into the Data Editor and weight the cells by the frequencies of cases in them.

Table 31.1   A three-way contingency showing the relationship between sex, sexual abuse and physical abuse in a sample of psychiatric hospital patients

Sexual abuse	Physical abuse	Sex		Margin totals
		Female	Male	
Sexually abused	Physical abuse	20	30	50
	No physical	40	25	65
Not sexually abused	Physical abuse	35	55	90
	No physical	45	50	95
Margin totals		140	160	300

31.1 Log-linear analysis

Quick summary

Enter data

Analyze

Loglinear

Model Selection

First category variable (e.g. sex)

▶

Define Range . . .

1

2

Continue

Repeat for further category variables (e.g. program)

OK

■ Enter the data in the Data Editor as shown in Figure 31.1. Label and weight the data.

	sexual	physical	sex	freq
1	1	1	1	20
2	1	1	2	30
3	1	2	1	40
4	1	2	2	25
5	2	1	1	35
6	2	1	2	55
7	2	2	1	45
8	2	2	2	50

Figure 31.1   **Weighted cases in the Data Editor**

- Select 'Analyze' from the menu bar near the top of the window which produces a drop-down menu (Figure 1.9).

- Select 'Loglinear' from the drop-down menu which reveals a smaller drop-down menu.

- Select 'Model Selection . . .' from this drop-down menu which opens the Model Selection Loglinear Analysis dialog box (Figure 31.2).

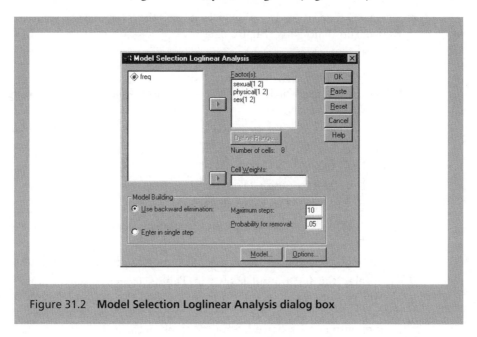

Figure 31.2   **Model Selection Loglinear Analysis dialog box**

- Select 'sexual' and then the ▶ button which puts 'sexual' in the 'Factors:' text box.

- Select 'Define Range . . .' which opens the 'Loglinear Analysis: Define Range' sub-dialog box (Figure 31.3).

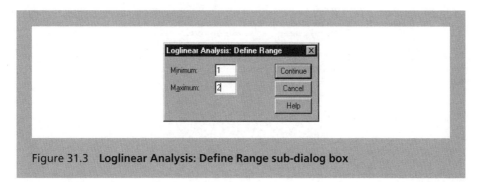

Figure 31.3   **Loglinear Analysis: Define Range sub-dialog box**

■ Type '1' in the box beside 'Minimum'.

■ Select box beside 'Maximum' and type '2'.

■ Select 'Continue' which closes the 'Loglinear Analysis: Define Range' sub-dialog box.

■ Select 'physical' and then the ▶ button which puts 'physical' in the 'Factors:' text box.

■ Select 'Define Range . . .' which opens the 'Loglinear Analysis: Define Range' sub-dialog box (Figure 31.3).

■ Type '1' in the box beside 'Minimum'.

■ Select box beside 'Maximum' and type '2'.

■ Select 'Continue' which closes the 'Loglinear Analysis: Define Range' sub-dialog box.

■ Select 'sex' and then the ▶ button which puts 'sex' in the 'Factors:' text box.

■ Select 'Define Range . . .' which opens the 'Loglinear Analysis: Define Range' sub-dialog box (Figure 31.3).

■ Type '1' in the box beside 'Minimum'.

■ Select box beside 'Maximum' and type '2'.

■ Select 'Continue' which closes the 'Loglinear Analysis: Define Range' sub-dialog box.

■ Select 'OK' which closes the 'Model Selection Loglinear Analysis' dialog box.

■ To display the full output shown in Table 31.2, click on the output in the Viewer window which creates a frame around the output (Figure 31.4). The down-pointing arrow at the lower left corner of the output indicates that there is more output to be viewed. Put the cursor on the little square in the centre of the bottom line and drag this line down until all the output is presented.

Table 31.2 **Hierarchical log-linear output**

```
* * * * * * * * * * *   H I E R A R C H I C A L   L O G   L I N E A R   * * * * * * * * * * *

DATA    Information

            8 unweighted cases accepted.
            0 cases rejected because of out-of-range factor values.
            0 cases rejected because of missing data.
          300 weighted cases will be used in the analysis.

FACTOR  Information

        Factor  Level  Label
        SEXUAL      2  Sexual abuse
        PHYSICAL    2  Physical abuse
        SEX         2  Sex

----------------------------------------------------------------------
```

```
* * * * * * * * * * *   H I E R A R C H I C A L   L O G   L I N E A R   * * * * * * * * * * *
```

DESIGN 1 has generating class

    SEXUAL*PHYSICAL*SEX

    Note: For saturated models   .500 has been added to all observed cells.
    This value may be changed by using the CRITERIA = DELTA subcommand.

The Iterative Proportional Fit algorithm converged at iteration 1.
The maximum difference between observed and fitted marginal totals is .000
and the convergence criterion is   .250

Observed, Expected Frequencies and Residuals.

Factor	Code	OBS count	EXP count	Residual	Std Resid
SEXUAL	Sexually				
PHYSICAL	Physical				
SEX	Females	20.5	20.5	.00	.00
SEX	Males	30.5	30.5	.00	.00
PHYSICAL	Not phys				
SEX	Females	40.5	40.5	.00	.00
SEX	Males	25.5	25.5	.00	.00
SEXUAL	Not sexu				
PHYSICAL	Physical				
SEX	Females	35.5	35.5	.00	.00
SEX	Males	55.5	55.5	.00	.00
PHYSICAL	Not phys				
SEX	Females	45.5	45.5	.00	.00
SEX	Males	50.5	50.5	.00	.00

  Goodness-of-fit test statistics

    Likelihood ratio chi square =   .00000   DF = 0   P = 1.000
                Pearson chi square =   .00000   DF = 0   P = 1.000

```
* * * * * * * * * * *   H I E R A R C H I C A L   L O G   L I N E A R   * * * * * * * * * * *
```

Tests that K-way and higher order effects are zero.

K	DF	L.R. Chisq	Prob	Pearson Chisq	Prob	Iteration
3	1	1.185	.2764	1.181	.2772	3
2	4	9.680	.0462	10.013	.0402	2
1	7	28.834	.0002	28.000	.0002	0

Tests that K-way effects are zero.

K	DF	L.R. Chisq	Prob	Pearson Chisq	Prob	Iteration
1	3	19.154	.0003	17.987	.0004	0
2	3	8.495	.0368	8.833	.0316	0
3	1	1.185	.2764	1.181	.2772	0

* * * * * * * * * * *   H I E R A R C H I C A L   L O G   L I N E A R   * * * * * * * * * * *

Backward Elimination (p = .050) for DESIGN 1 with generating class

    SEXUAL*PHYSICAL*SEX

  Likelihood ratio chi square =   .00000   DF = 0   P = 1.000

If Deleted Simple Effect is	DF	L.R. Chisq Change	Prob	Iter
SEXUAL*PHYSICAL*SEX	1	1.185	.2674	3

Step 1

  The best model has generating class

    SEXUAL*PHYSICAL
    SEXUAL*SEX
    PHYSICAL*SEX

Likelihood ratio chi square =   1.18471   DF = 1   P = .276

If Deleted Simple Effect is	DF	L.R. Chisq Change	Prob	Iter
SEXUAL*PHYSICAL*SEX	1	.454	.5005	2
SEXUAL*SEX	1	1.963	.1612	2
PHYSICAL*SEX	1	5.461	.0194	2

Step 2

  The best model has generating class

    SEXUAL*SEX
    PHYSICAL*SEX

Likelihood ratio chi square =   1.63849   DF = 2   P = .441

If Deleted Simple Effect is	DF	L.R. Chisq Change	Prob	Iter
SEXUAL*SEX	1	2.272	.1317	2
PHYSICAL*SEX	1	5.770	.0163	2

```
* * * * * * * * * * *   H I E R A R C H I C A L   L O G   L I N E A R   * * * * * * * * * * *
```

Step 3

  The best model has generating class

    PHYSICAL*SEX
    SEXUAL

Likelihood ratio chi square =   3.91036   DF = 3 P = .271

- -

If Deleted Simple Effect is   DF   L.R. Chisq Change   Prob   Iter

  PHYSICAL*SEX   1   5.770   .0163   2
  SEXUAL   1   16.485   .0000   2

Step 4

  The best model has generating class

    PHYSICAL*SEX
    SEXUAL

Likelihood ratio chi square =   3.91036   DF = 3 P = .271

- -

```
* * * * * * * * * * *   H I E R A R C H I C A L   L O G   L I N E A R   * * * * * * * * * * *
```

The final model has generating class

    PHYSICAL*SEX
    SEXUAL

The Iterative Proportional Fit algorithm converged at iteration 0.
The maximum difference between observed and fitted marginal totals is   .000
and the convergence criterion is   .250

- -

Observed, Expected Frequencies and Residuals.

Factor	Code	OBS count	EXP count	Residual	Std Resid
SEXUAL	Sexually				
PHYSICAL	Physical				
SEX	Females	20.0	21.1	−1.08	−.24
SEX	Males	30.0	32.6	−2.58	−.45
PHYSICAL	Not phys				
SEX	Females	40.0	32.6	7.42	1.30
SEX	Males	25.0	28.8	−3.75	−.70

```
SEXUAL       Not sexu
  PHYSICAL     Physical
      SEX          Females       35.0        35.9        1.08         .19
      SEX          Males         55.0        52.4        2.58         .36
  PHYSICAL     Not phys
      SEX          Females       45.0        52.4       -7.42       -1.02
      SEX          Males         50.0        46.3        3.75         .55


- - - - - - - - - - - - - - - - - - - - - - - - - - - - - - - - - - - - - - - - -

  Goodness-of-fit test statistics

     Likelihood ratio chi square =      3.91036    DF = 3  P = .271
                 Pearson chi square =      3.95320    DF = 3  P = .267


- - - - - - - - - - - - - - - - - - - - - - - - - - - - - - - - - - - - - - - - -
```

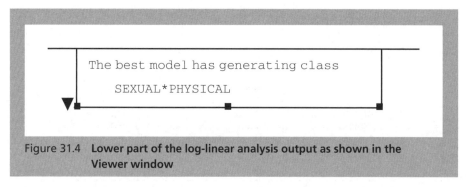

The best model has generating class

SEXUAL*PHYSICAL

Figure 31.4   **Lower part of the log-linear analysis output as shown in the Viewer window**

31.2 Interpreting the output in Table 31.2

- There are two statistics used to test the goodness-of-fit of the various models. These are the likelihood ratio Chi-square and Pearson Chi-square. The likelihood ratio Chi-square is the test more commonly used because it has the advantage of being linear so Chi-square values may be added or subtracted.

- The likelihood ratio Chi-square for the saturated or full model is presented first and is .00000 which has a probability of 1.000. In other words, the saturated model provides a perfect fit for the observed frequencies and so is non-significant. The saturated model in this case consists of the three main effects, three two-way interactions and one three-way interaction. In general, the saturated model includes all main effects and interactions.

- However, the saturated model includes ALL components whether or not they individually contribute to explaining the variation in the observed data. So it is necessary to eliminate components in turn to see whether this makes the model's fit worse. If it does, this component of the model is kept for the final model.

- SPSS begins with the full model and eliminates each effect in turn to determine which effects make the least significant change in the likelihood ratio

Chi-square. The best-fitting model is presented last. In our example, this includes the interaction of physical abuse and sex and the main effect of sexual abuse. This model has a likelihood ratio Chi-square of 3.91 (rounded to two decimal places), 2 degrees of freedom and a probability level of .271. In other words, it is not significant which means that the observed data can be reproduced with these two effects.

■ To interpret these two effects, we need to present the data in terms of a one-way table for sexual abuse and a two-way table for physical abuse and sex. We can do this using Chi-square . . . for the one-way table and Crosstabs . . . for the two-way table. These two tables are shown in Table 31.3. The one-way table shows that more psychiatric patients have not been sexually abused than have been sexually abused. The two-way table indicates that males are more likely to be physically abused than females.

Table 31.3 **Contingency tables for sexual abuse and the interaction of physical abuse and sex**

Sexual abuse

	Observed N	Expected N	Residual
Sexually abused	115	150.0	−35.0
Not sexually abused	185	150.0	35.0
Total	300		

Physical abuse * Sex Crosstabulation

			Sex		Total
			Females	Males	
Physical abuse	Physically abused	Count	55	85	140
		Expected Count	65.3	74.7	140.0
		Residual	−10.3	10.3	
	Not physically abused	Count	85	75	160
		Expected Count	74.7	85.3	160.0
		Residual	10.3	−10.3	
Total		Count	140	160	300
		Expected Count	140.0	160.0	300.0

■ It is possible to see the contribution of each component to the final model. Just before the final step (Step 4 in this example), there is a small table headed 'If Deleted Simple Effect is'. This contains a column called 'L.R. Chisq Change'. These entries essentially indicate the change (reduction) in the goodness-of-fit Chi-square if each component is taken away. Thus PHYSI-

CAL*SEX has a L.R. Chi-Square Change of 5.770 which is significant (.0163). SEXUAL has a value of 16.485 which is very significant (.0000). Obviously these two effects cannot be eliminated from the model because of their significant contribution.

■ In a hierarchical model, components of an interaction may be significant. Since PHYSICAL*SEX has a significant contribution to the model, PHYSICAL and SEX may themselves be significant main effects. Select 'Model' in the Model Selection Loglinear Analysis dialog box (Figure 31.2). The window that appears will allow you to test these main effects by stipulating models containing only these particular main effects.

31.3 Reporting the results of Table 31.2

■ One way of describing the results found here is as follows: "A three-way frequency analysis was performed to develop a hierarchical linear model of physical and sexual abuse in female and male psychiatric patients. Backward elimination produced a model that included the main effect of sexual abuse and the interaction effect of physical abuse and sex. The model had a likelihood ratio $\chi^2(3) = 3.91$, $p = .27$, indicating a good fit between the observed frequencies and the expected frequencies generated by the model. About 38 per cent of the psychiatric patients had been sexually abused. About 53 per cent of the males had been physically abused compared with about 39 per cent of the females.".

Supplement 1

SPSS Release 8 for Windows

■ *Release 8 lacks the 'Data View' and 'Variable View' features of the Data Editor ('spreadsheet'). This is the really important change with Release 10.*

■ *Release 8 uses the word Statistics on the tool bar whereas Analyze is used in Releases 9 and 10.*

■ *In Release 8 the sub-menu for Statistics uses the term Summarize. This was changed to Descriptive Statistics in Releases 9 and 10.*

■ *Release 8 differs in that 'GLM – General Factorial' is used on General Linear Model sub-window instead of the term 'Univariate' (as in Releases 9 and 10).*

■ *Similarly, for the mixed design ANOVA, the term 'GLM – Repeated Measures' is used instead of 'Repeated Measures' as in Releases 9 and 10.*

■ *The following instructions should replace sections 2.2, 2.3, 15.2 and 25.2 if you are using Releases 8 or 9.*

2.2   Labelling variables and their values

■ Select the first column (i.e. make sure your cursor or the active cell which is enframed in bold is in the first column).

■ Select 'Data' from the menu bar towards the top of the window which produces a drop-down menu.

■ Select 'Define Variable . . .' which opens the Define Variable dialog box.

■ Check that the selected variable is the correct one (i.e. var00001 in our example). We will call 'var00001' 'occupat' by typing in 'Occupat' which will delete the highlighted default name 'var00001' in the 'Variable Name:' box.

■ Select 'Labels . . .' which opens the 'Define Labels' sub-dialog box.

- We can give a longer version of the column name which will only be displayed in the output by typing this name in the 'Variable Label:' box. So type in the longer name of 'Occupation'.
- Select 'Value:' in the Value Labels section and type '1' in the box beside it.
- Select box beside 'Value Label:' and type 'Nun' in it.
- Select 'Add' which puts 1.00 = 'Nuns' in the bottom box.
- Repeat this procedure for the remaining four values and labels as shown in Figure 2.5.
- Select 'Continue' which closes the 'Define Labels' sub-dialog box.
- Select 'OK' which closes the Define Variable dialog box. The first column in the Data Editor is now labelled 'occupat'.

2.3   Omitting decimal places in whole numbers

- Select the first column.
- Select 'Data' from the menu bar towards the top of the window which produces a drop-down menu.
- Select 'Define Variable . . .' which opens the Define Variable dialog box.
- Select 'Type . . .' which opens the 'Define Variable Type' sub-dialog box.
- Highlight the '2' in the box beside 'Decimal Places:' and type '0'.
- Select 'Continue' which closes the 'Define Variable Type' sub-dialog box.
- Select 'OK', which closes the Define Variable dialog box. The data in the first column of the Data Editor no longer have two zero decimal places.

15.2 Defining missing values

- To code missing values for a variable, put the cursor anywhere in the Data Editor column which holds the values of that variable. So, to code missing values for the music test put the cursor in the first column.
- Select 'Data' from the menu bar near the top of the window which produces a drop-down menu.
- Select 'Define Variable . . .' which opens the Define Variable dialog box.
- Select 'Missing Values . . .' in the Change Settings section which opens the 'Define Missing Values' sub-dialog box.
- Select 'Discrete missing values' and type '11' in the first box.
- Select 'Continue' which closes the 'Define Missing Values' sub-dialog box and which puts '11' besides 'Missing Values' in the Variable Description section.

■ Select 'OK', which closes the Define Variable dialog box and opens the Data Editor window.

25.2 Reading an ASCII data file

■ Select 'File' from the menu bar near the top of the window to produce a drop-down menu.

■ Select 'Read ASCII Data' which opens a drop-down menu with two options.

■ Select 'Fixed Columns' which opens the Define Fixed Variables dialog box.

■ Select 'Browse . . .' which opens the 'Define Fixed Variables: Browse' sub-dialog box.

■ If you know the file name and its location, type in the disk drive, directory (if any) and file name of the ASCII data file (e.g. 'a:dat.txt') in the box beside 'File name:' and select 'Open' which closes the 'Define Fixed Variables: Browse' sub-dialog box and returns you to the Define Fixed Variables dialog box. If you are uncertain of the file name and/or its location, select the 'Look in:' box whic opens a drop-down menu with different locations on it. Note that if the name of your file does not end with the suffix '.dat', you need to select 'All files[*.*]' in the box beside 'Files of type:' to show files ending with this suffix. Once you have found the file name, select it and then 'Open'.

■ In the 'Name:' box type the SPSS name of the first variable to be defined. As the rows of the Data Editor are already numbered, the name of the first variable to be defined is 'gender'.

■ The column in which 'gender' is stored is column 2. As there is only one column for 'gender', the number to be put in the 'Start Column:' box is the same as the number for the 'End Column:' box. Consequently, it is only necessary to put 2 in the 'Start Column:' box. Select the 'Start Column:' box and type '2'.

■ Select 'Add' which puts '1 2- 2 gender' in the 'Defined Variables:' box.

■ Type in the 'Name:' box the SPSS name of the next variable to be defined which is 'age'.

■ Select the 'Start Column:' box and type '3'.

■ Select the 'End Column:' box and type '4'.

■ Select 'Add' which puts '2 3- 4 age' in the 'Defined Variables:' box.

■ After all the required variables have been defined select 'OK' which closes the Define Fixed Variables dialog box and opens the Data Editor window which now contains the SPSS variable names and values of the ASCII data file.

Supplement 2

SPSS Release 9 for Windows

■ Release 9 lacks the 'Data View' and 'Variable View' features of the Data Editor ('spreadsheet'). This is the really important change with Release 10. In this respect it is like Release 8 in terms of labelling variables, stipulating decimal places and so forth. The procedure for reading ASCII text files also differs. See SPSS Release 8 for Windows Supplement for instructions.

SPSS Release 10 for Windows

■ Changes are minor between Release 10 and Release 11 of SPSS as far as the contents of this guide are concerned. The only differences seem to be in the way aspects of the correlation coefficient output are reported. Thus pages 74, 76 and 207 in this text are slightly different from Release 11 output. The correlation of a variable with itself is reported as 1 in Release 11 and no significance level is reported. Most users will not notice the changes.

Appendix A

Confidence intervals

■ *Confidence intervals are far from new in statistics but have recently been advocated as preferable to the sorts of point estimates commonly used in most statistical analyses. The mean of a sample can be used as an estimate of the mean of the population from which that sample was taken. This single estimate is a point estimate of the population mean since it is expressed as a single value such as 5.3. However, we know that this estimate based on a sample is merely the best one and that the actual population mean is likely to be different from this estimate.*

■ *In confidence intervals, the estimated mean is expressed in terms of a range of means within which the actual population mean is likely to lie. Thus the confidence interval for a mean may be 4.2 to 6.4.*

■ *The confidence interval will vary according to the level of certainty required by the researcher. So, for the same data, the confidence interval to be 95% likely to include the population mean is narrower than the confidence interval to be 99% likely to include the population mean.*

■ *Earlier in this book we have used confidence intervals when they seem particularly useful. One of the difficulties with the confidence interval approach lies in the fact that any statistic theoretically has a confidence interval. Despite this, it is difficult to find the methods for calculating them in the statistical literature and textbooks. This limits the applicability of the confidence interval approach. More to the point here, SPSS in common with all computer programs only provides a limited number of confidence intervals.*

Confidence intervals have been presented in the output for the following tests described in this book:

Regression – *B*: Table 8.2 (second table)
Related *t*-test: Table 12.2 (third table)

Unrelated *t*-test: Table 13.2 (second table)
One-way unrelated ANOVA: Table 20.2 (first table)
Two-way unrelated ANOVA: Table 22.2 (last three tables)
Multiple-comparison tests: Table 23.2 (second table)
One-way ANCOVA: Table 24.2 (fourth table)

Confidence intervals can also be readily obtained for the following statistics:

One-sample *t*-test
One-way related ANOVA
Two-way mixed ANOVA
Regression – predicted score

Appendix B

Other statistics on SPSS

Other statistical tests provided by SPSS but not described in this book are shown below in terms of their options on the Statistics menu, submenu and dialog box options.

Statistics menu	Statistics submenu	Dialog box
Descriptive Statistics	Crosstabs . . .	Lambda
		Uncertainty coefficient
		Gamma
		Somers' d
		Kendall's tau-b
		Kendall's tau-c
		Risk
		Eta
Correlate	Bivariate . . .	Kendall's tau-b
Regression	Curve Estimation . . .	
	Binary Logistic . . .	
	Multinomial Logistic . . .	
	Ordinal . . .	
	Probit . . .	
	Nonlinear . . .	
	Weight Estimation . . .	
	2-Stage Least Squares . . .	
	Optimal Scaling . . .	
Loglinear	Logit . . .	
Classify	K-Means Cluster . . .	
	Hierarchical Cluster . . .	
	Discriminant . . .	

Data Reduction	Correspondence Analysis . . .	
	Optimal Scaling . . .	
Scale	Multidimensional Scaling . . .	
	Multidimensional Scaling[PROXSCAL] . . .	
Nonparametric Tests	Binomial . . .	
	Runs . . .	
	1-Sample K-S . . . (Kolmogorov–Smirnov)	
	2 Independent Samples . . .	Kolmogorov–Smirnov Z
		Wald–Wolfowitz runs
		Moses extreme reactions
	K Independent Samples . . .	Kruskal–Wallis H
		Jonckheere–Terpstra
		Median
	2 Related Samples . . .	Marginal Homogeneity
	K Related Samples . . .	Friedman
		Kendall's W
		Cochran's Q
Time Series	Exponential Smoothing . . .	
	Autoregression . . .	
	ARIMA . . .	
	Seasonal Decomposition . . .	
Survival	Life Tables . . .	
	Kaplan–Meier . . .	
	Cox Regression . . .	
	Cox w/ Time-Dep Cov . . .	

Index